ETHNIC CHRONOLOGY SERIES
NUMBER 22

Ref
E184
P8
C36

The Portuguese in America 590 B.C. -1974

A Chronology & Fact Book

Compiled and edited by

Soares

Manoel da Silveira Cardozo

1976
OCEANA PUBLICATIONS, INC.
DOBBS FERRY, NEW YORK

Library of Congress Cataloging in Publication Data

Cardozo, Manoel da Silveira Soares, 1911-
  The Portuguese in America, 590 B.C. - 1976.

    (Ethnic chronology series; no. 24)
    Bibliography: p.
    Includes index.
    SUMMARY: A chronology of the Portuguese in America
accompanied by pertinent documents.
    1. Portuguese Americans. [1. Portuguese Americans]
  I. Title. II. Series.
  E184.P8C36   973'.04'691   75-45203
  ISBN 0-379-00520-4

Manufactured in the United States of America

TABLE OF CONTENTS

INTRODUCTION

This is hardly the definitive work on the Portuguese in America. Much more research and reflection will have to be done before a more exhaustive book can be written. But, until such time, the present volume will serve as an easy source of ready reference and, for those sensitive enough to perceive the symbolism of certain emphases and juxtapositions of data, something more than the mere record of a humane experience will suggest itself. Other collections have done the same thing but not in the same way, or so soon, or with the same intensity.

The texts that follow the Chronology are transcripts of documents that have a bearing upon our story, in real or symbolic ways. Whenever additional material is given, to complete or enlarge upon the information supplied by the document itself, brackets are used to separate one from the other.

The studies are of a different nature. They were written by the author and treat subjects or persons that could not have been covered or treated in another fashion. They appear interspersed with the texts, without a generic label, but the reader will have no trouble in telling them apart.

The statistical section is purposely limited, largely because figures on the Portuguese are not to be trusted.

As to the bibliography, it is not meant to be comprehensive but essentially a listing of the source that I have used. And finally, unless otherwise indicated, all translations are mine.

The reader should also be told that the story as outlined below does not concern itself exclusively with the Portuguese in the United States and its possessions or with the Portuguese within the existing territorial limits of the United States. For purposes of balance, and to point up the extent of Portuguese migration in the past, I have touched upon the larger Portuguese presence on the American continents. I wanted to show, however succinctly, that the Portuguese at one time in their history swarmed over the globe, and that their coming to the United States, when seen in this light, was not a departure in principle from the ancient wandering propensitites of the race.

From the vast geographical area of the Americas, as I have covered it in these pages, I have consciously excluded Portuguese America. Brazil was the supreme achievement of the Portuguese colonial effort in the Western Hemisphere, but I am interested only in the Portuguese under foreign jurisdiction. Brazil was not foreign to them. It belonged to them. And it offered the Portuguese who went there privileged conditions for settlement. Elsewhere on these continents, and especially in the United States, which is the focus of the book, the Portuguese were no longer at home but under the control of other powers. How the Portuguese, unprotected by the sovereignty of their own crown, survived and flourised on alien soil is not the least revealing of the lessons to be learned in subsequent pages.

With the needs of the book in mind, I have defined the Portuguese nation in the broadest possible terms. I have not circumscribed it to Catholics, even though they have always formed the overwhelming majority of the population, or to Europeans from the Iberian homeland. I have placed everybody under the Portuguese umbrella: Catholics, Sephardim, Protestants, mainlanders, Azoreans, Madeirans, and Cape Verdeans. In the past, certain component parts of the nation have not always lived at peace with the dominant culture, but there is no reason why they should not now be brought together in their transatlantic context.

The history of the Portuguese presence in America may be roughly divided into two periods, before and after the Civil War, which comprise nontheless a continuing whole, from the legendary (and certainly fantastic) beginnings in classical times to a song in an Acushnet, Massachusetts, restaurant that brings 1974 to a close. The earlier achievements were different from the later ones, and the dimensions are quite unique, but the divisions of time are part of the larger whole, and the happenings in each must be seen in the same way.

No European people has been longer in the New World or more continuously than the Portuguese. Perhaps this is the way it was meant to be. After all, they have proportionately furnished more immigrants to the Western World than any other nation of Europe (with the possible exception of England). Having established the first of the modern colonial empires, and on virtually all the continents of the world, this errant race, not content with the enormity of its own geographical space, also emigrated to lands under the control of other sovereignties.

The two great Portuguese communities in the United States, one in New England and the other in California, both created substantially within the past 100 years, are separated by distance, by climate, and in some ways by occupation too. There used to be considerable communication between them, when family ties were stronger, but as they have settled in they have also settled down. The same relative isolation is the lot of the smaller communities elsewhere in the country.

This book, the first of its kind, is intended to put it all together, and the chronological format is admirably suited for its purposes. I say this because Portugal and the Portuguese have been unflatteringly treated by the English-speaking world since the Reformation. The sober record of achievement, without any obvious conceptualizing, will therefore dispell misinformation and help remove cobwebs of prejudice. To that extent it will contribute to a more harmonious republic, where understanding overcomes suspicion.

590 B.C.   Carthaginian merchants sailed westward from the Iberian peninsula to the Antilles and New Spain, according to Gaspar Frutuoso (1522-1591), the Azorean chronicler of the Atlantic Islands. There are references in Frutuoso as well as in Damião de Góis (1502-1574), the Portuguese humanist who chronicled the reign of King Emmanuel I (1495-1521), to a stone statue of a man pointing westward on the Azorean island of Corvo. Both declared that it was erected by Phoenician or Carthaginian adventurers on a spot that later was found to be only 1,054 miles from Newfoundland.

734 A.D.   Martin Behaim (1459-1507), the German geographer, wrote on his Nuremberg globe of 1492 that in 734, following the conquest of Iberia by the Muslims from North Africa, the island of Antilia was discovered and settled by an archbishop of Oporto, Portugal, who fled to it in ships with six fellow bishops and other Christians, and there built Seven Cities.

1325   The Genoese map of Dalcorto placed the island of Brazil to the west of Ireland. This was a mythical island dear to the imagination of medieval cartographers, not the Land of the True Cross, or modern Brazil, which the Portuguese navigator, Pedro Álvares Cabral, reached on his way to India via the Cape of Good Hope on April 22, 1500.

1415   King John I of Portugal (1357-1433), the father of Prince Henry the Navigator, conquered Ceuta on the North African coast across from Gibraltar. He began in this way the expansion of Portugal overseas and opened the modern period of European history.

1425   João Gonçalves Zarco, under the authority of Prince Henry the Navigator, began the colonization of Madeira. The island, some 500 miles west of the Moroccan coast, was uninhabited when the Portuguese got there. Madeira early based its economy on the raising of sugarcane and on the production of wine. As early as the sixteenth century, Gaspar Frutuoso, the chronicler of the Atlantic Islands, called the wine of Madeira the best in the world.

1431   Martin Behaim declared on his Nuremberg globe of 1492 that the Portuguese reached the Azores in 1431 and in 1432 left domestic animals on the islands to breed and multiply. Towards the end of the sixteenth century, Gaspar Frutuoso wrote that the island of Santa Maria was discovered in 1432 by Friar Gonçalo Velho Cabral, a knight of the Military Order of Christ (of which Prince Henry the Navigator was governor or administrator). The Azores were virtually midway between Europe and North America. Santa Maria is 870 miles west of Lisbon; Corvo is 1,054 miles eas of Cape Race, Newfoundland.

1439   Prince Henry the Navigator authorized the colonization of the Azores. The earliest settlement was brought about under the leadership of Gonçalo Velho Cabral, who brought colonists from Portugal. Other colonists came from Flanders, sent by Elizabeth, Duchess of Burgundy, the sister of Prince Henry. The colonization of the Azores was achieved very quickly, enabling the archipelago to take a part in the Age of Discovery. Vasco da Gama, on his return from his great voyage to India (1497-1499), stopped at Terceira, where his brother Paulo died and was buried. A few years later a number of expeditions sailed from the Azores to the maritime provinces of Canada. The Spanish commercial convoys from Veracruz and Havana rendezvoused in Terceira, as did the Portuguese convoys from Brazil, joined by carracks from India and China.

1455   The Genoese Antonio da Noli may have discovered five of the islands of the Cape Verde archipelago in July. The Venetian Alvisi Cadamosto reached the same islands in May, 1456. Both Italians were on Portuguese expeditions. The northwestern cluster of islands was discovered by Diogo Afonso, a Portuguese, possibly between December and January, 1461-1462.

1457   Bartolomeu Perestrelo, a native of Piacenza, Italy, and since 1446 donatary of Porto Santo in the Madeiran archipelago, died on or about this year on his island. He is remembered in history as the father-in-law of Christopher Columbus, the discoverer of the New World, who spent some some time in Madeira and married Perestrelo's daughter, Filipa Moniz de Melo, in Lisbon in 1479. Columbus' only legitimate child, Diogo, was born from this union. When the mother died in Funchal about the year 1485, little did she know that her grandson, the heir to the Columbus name, would become the first Duke of Veragua and the first Marquess of Jamaica in the Castilian peerage.

1492   On Columbus' voyage of discovery, five men and boys out of the ninety members of the crew, including the admiral himself, were foreigners. One of the foreigners has been identified as a Portuguese with the Hispanic name of Juan Arias, and he is said to have hailed from "Tavaria" in Portugal. Translated into Portuguese, Juan Arias must be João Aires and Tavaria, Tavira, next door to Palos, whither Columbus sailed in 1492. It is interesting to point out that Christopher Columbus, when he discovered the New World, was more fluent in Portuguese than he was in Castilian.

1493   On his return trip to Spain from America, Columbus first stopped in two Portuguese ports: in Santa Maria, Azores, on February 13, and Lisbon, March 4. The Portuguese were the first to know of the success of the undertaking.

Pope Alexander VI obliged the Catholic kings of Castile and Aragon by declaring that Castile was entitled to all lands west of a line drawn from pole 100 leagues beyond the Azores and the Cape Verde Islands, and Portugal to lands east of it. The unwillingness of the Portuguese to accept the Pope's decision led to the Treaty of Tordesillas of June 7, 1494, confirmed by Pope Julius II on January 24, 1506, by means of which the line of demarcation was moved farther to the west, a total of 370 leagues beyond the Cape Verde Islands.

1496   March 5. Henry VII of England granted letters-patent to John Cabot and his three sons authorizing them to sail anywhere "under our banners and ensignes" to discover the lands of the "heathen and infidelles." The English letters-patent followed the form of the charters that the Portuguese kings had been granting their subjects under similar circumstances.

1500   The first quarter of the sixteenth-century, according to Samuel Eliot Morison, the historian of discovery, was "an era of Portuguese supremacy in exploration of the north, and of other nations gradually getting on to the wonderful fishing" in the Newfoundland area and the Grand Banks. The maps of those days show how extensive Portuguese involvement was in these northern lands and waters.

April 22. Pedro Álvares Cabral, in command of a powerful expedition that was scheduled to go to India via the Cape of Good Hope, reached South America and claimed Brazil for the Crown of Portugal.

During the summer of 1500, Gaspar Corte-Real left Lisbon

on his second voyage to North America. From Greenland, he sailed on to Labrador, where he turned south. He erected a padrão, or mark of possession, at the mouth of the Alexis River. He then continued to Newfoundland. Two of the three ships of his expedition returned to Lisbon in October. The third ship, with Gaspar on board, was never heard from again.

In the course of the second Corte-Real expedition, the Portuguese are supposed to have ascended the St. Lawrence River, mistaking it for a passage to the Pacific Ocean, and indirectly, and in a fit of pique, given Canada its name. ". . . on arriving at the point where they ascertained that it was not a strait, but a river, they, with all the emphasis of disappointed hopes, exclaimed repeatedly, Cà, nada! -- (here, nothing!) which words caught the attention of the natives, and were remembered and repeated by them on seeing other Europeans, under Jacques Cartier, arrive in 1534, -- but Cartier mistakes the object of the Portuguese to have been gold mines, not a passage to India; and if the Portuguese account be true, he also mistook the exclamation of Cà, nada, for the name of the country."

Amerigo Vespucci, the Italian seaman after whom the New World is called, sailed on a Portuguese expedition to the coast of South America.

1502   May 10. Miguel Corte-Real left Lisbon to look for his lost brother Gaspar. In January the King of Portugal had transferred to him half of what Gaspar was thought to own in Newfoundland. The expedition reached St. John's River, which he named, probably in June. Gaspar's mysterious fate was reserved for Miguel: his ship was also lost.

Cape Race, Newfoundland, is called by its Portuguese name of Cabo Raso in the King chart.

The earliest Portuguese map of North America is named after Alberto Cantino, the agent of Duke Ercole d'Este, who sent it to him from Lisbon. The map, in the style of the portulans of the fifteenth century, shows Greenland, the Corte-Real voyages to Newfoundland, and an unidentified voyage of discovery to Florida antedating the generally accepted discovery of 1513 by Juan Ponce de León. The map also records the Pedro Álvares Cabral landfall of 1500 in Brazil.

1505   Azoreans took "popyngais and catts of the mountaigne"
            from Newfoundland to England.

1508   The John Ruysch map identifies Cape Race, Newfoundland,
            as the Cape of the Portuguese.

1511   Professor Edmund B. Delabarre of Brown University de-
            clared in 1926 that he had found a Portuguese coat-of-arms
            with the date of 1511 and the inscription "Migvel Cortereal
            V Dei Hic Dux Ind" on the Dighton Rock, located on the left
            bank of the Taunton River 30 miles from the mouth of Nar-
            ragansett Bay within the town limits of Berkley, Massachu-
            setts. Delabarre theorized that Miguel, shipwrecked on
            his voyage of 1502, made his way to Assonet Neck, became
            chief of the Wampanoag, and died in 1511, having earlier
            been, by the will of God, chief of the Indians. The marker
            was ostensibly set up by faithful followers to commemorate
            his death. Dr. Manuel Luciano da Silva, a prominent phy-
            sician of Bristol, Rhode Island, and a leader of the Portu-
            guese community in New England, defended the Delabarre
            interpretation in his book, Portuguese Pilgrims and Dighton
            Rock, edited by Nelson T. Martins and privately published
            in Bristol in 1971. (A Portuguese edition, published in Lis-
            bon, appeared in 1974.) Samuel Eliot Morison, the Ameri-
            can historian of discovery, takes a contrary view. If Dela-
            barre is correct, a Portuguese was the first European to
            settle in New England.

1514   Dom Nuno Manuel, a Portuguese, explored the Río de la
            Plata and gave the great estuary of South America its name.

1516   One of the chief characters of St. Thomas More's Utopia
            is the Portuguese sailor Ralph Hytholoday.

            A renegade Portuguese in the service of Castile, João Dias
            de Solís, commanded an expedition that reached the Río de
            la Plata. A number of fellow Portuguese accompanied him.

1519-22   Ferdinand Magellan (Fernão de Magalhães), the Portuguese
            navigator in the service of Castile who was the first to cir-
            cumnavigate the globe, left Spain in 1519 and was killed in
            the Philippines in 1521. Elcano reached Spain, now over
            charted routes, in 1522. Three captains of the expedition
            and their pilots were Portuguese. The chief pilot was also
            Portuguese, Estêvão Gomes, who abandoned the expedition
            at the Straits of Magellan and returned to Spain. Magellan
            named Montevideo, Patagonia, and the Pacific Ocean.

1520

A Portuguese ship's carpenter, Álvaro Fernandes, was on Pánfilo de Narváez's expedition to the coast of Mexico.

João Álvares Fagundes, a Portuguese, sailed along the south coast of Newfoundland and ventured into the Gulf of St. Lawrence. He named the principal places that he discovered, including Penguin Island. He discovered St. Pierre and Miquelon and the islets that lie between them and Newfoundland, and set up a permanent shore establishment a century before the English. Colonists were recruited in the northern Portuguese province of Minho, where he was born, and in the Azores. They crossed the Atlantic between 1521 and 1523 and settled on Cape Breton Island. When the Indians became hostile, Fagundes and his people moved south along the coast of Nova Scotia. He discovered the Bay of Fundy and apparently settled the group there. "By 1526, perhaps before, this earliest (save the Norsemen's) of many vain attempts of Europeans to set up a colony in North America no longer existed. . . ." (Samuel Eliot Morison).

1521

August 13. The Aztec capital, Tenochtitlán, upon whose ruins Mexico City was built, fell to Hernán Cortés, the Spanish conquistador. There were eight Portuguese in the Spanish forces.

1524-25

Aleixo Garcia, the unsung Portuguese pioneer of South America, who crossed the continent from the Atlantic to Paraguay, antedated by seventeen years the more famous overland march through the same territory of Alvar Núñez Cabeza de Vaca, by four years Sebastian Cabot's discovery of the Paraguay River, by thirteen years Juan de Ayolas' exploration of the Chaco, and by thirteen years the first appearance of Francisco Pizarro's men in Charcas. The first white man to reach Paraguay and Bolivia, Garcia was killed by the Indians in 1525.

1525

Estévão Gomes, a native of Oporto and Magellan's chief pilot, was commissioned by the Emperor Charles V in 1523 to find a northwest passage between the Atlantic and Pacific. He sailed from La Coruña in September, 1524, and reached North America in February, 1525. Despite the winter weather, he entered the Gulf of St. Lawrence. He sighted Prince Edward Island, discovered the Gut of Canso, and followed the coasts of Nova Scotia and Maine. He sailed up the Penobscot looking for the illusive strait. It is likely that he reached Cape Cod, probably in July, 1525. He was back in Spain in August.

Diogo Dias, a stonecutter and sculptor from Lisbon, carved a corner window for the Hospital of Jesus the Nazarene of Mexico City, an institution founded by Hernán Cortés, the conqueror of the Aztec Empire. The window was destroyed in 1800.

1538   A Portuguese slaver reached Puerto Rico. This was the first Portuguese arribada in the Caribbean.

1539   May 30. Hernando de Soto, the Spanish explorer, landed near Tampa Bay, Florida, with 600 men. There seem to have been at least 100 Portuguese in his party. The expedition moved across Florida, Georgia, the Carolinas to the Appalachian Mountains, Alabama, Mississippi, Tennessee, Arkansas, and Oklahoma. After May 21, 1542, when De Soto died on the banks of the Mississippi River, the survivors went on to Texas. Among the victims of the Texas excursion was André de Vasconcelos da Silva, a nobleman from Elvas, Portugal. The chronicle of the amazing expedition, by the anonymous Fidalgo de Elvas, or Gentleman of Elvas, is in Portuguese. It is the oldest description of the territories covered.

1540   Francisco Vásquez de Coronado, governor of the New Kingdom of León, began the search for the Seven Cities of Cibola, whose existence had earlier been reported by a Franciscan friar, Marcos de Niza. There were no less than five Portuguese on the expedition, all horsemen: André do Campo, Gaspar Álvares, André Martins, Fernão Pais, and a person identified as Horta. The expedition visited New Mexico, Texas, Colorado, Oklahoma, Kansas, and Nebraska. Before the return to Mexico, Juan de Padilla, a Franciscan, decided to stay behind, to minister to the Indians of Quivira. The Portuguese André do Campo stayed with him. This was the first attempt to establish a Catholic mission without military support in the interior of the present-day territory of the United States. About nine years later, Campos and two Indian companions turned up in Pánuco, the old northeastern province of New Spain. "They had spent some years in their flight from Quivira, serving many months as slaves to the Indian tribes of the Mississippi basin, circling and cutting back, always striving to make their way to Mexico and their own people. Their tale of the death of Fray Juan de Padilla, protomartyr of the United States, is well worthy of a place in the calendar of saints" (A. Grove Day).

November 2. Alvar Núñez Cabeza de Vaca left Spain for
South America. He arrived in Santa Catarina, Brazil, on
March 29, 1541. On November 2, 1541, he began the over-
land journey to Asunción, Paraguay, taking the Portuguese
Gonçalo da Costa with him as interpreter and guide. The
party reached its destination on March 9, 1542.

1542

João Rodrigues Cabrilho, a Portuguese, arrived in Cuba
with Pedro de Alvarado in 1518. He was captain of a company of crossbowmen in the Pánfilo de Narváez expedition
that the governor of Cuba sent against Hernán Cortés in
1520, and thus took part in the historic conquest of Mexico.
He was later involved with the conquest of Oaxaca. He was
in Guatemala in 1540, outfitting a fleet to search for the
mythical Seven Cities. Antonio de Mendoza, the first viceroy of Mexico, appointed him to explore the northern Pacific
coast of New Spain. His two small vessels, the San Salvador and the Victoria entered the bay of San Miguel, now
San Diego, where, according to the log book kept by his
chief pilot, a fellow Portuguese by the name of Bartolomeu
Ferrer (or Ferrelo, as he is generally known), he took possession of those lands and waters in the name of the Emperor Charles V. California had been discovered by Europeans. Cabrilho reached Drake's Bay on November 14, 1542,
named Cape Mendocino after the viceroy of Mexico, and
died on January 3, 1543, on San Miguel Island, off the Santa
Barbara coast. The expedition now continued under Ferrer.
Charles E. Chapman, the historian of California, wrote
that the discovery of Alta California was achieved "under
conditions requiring a courage and tenacity that seem to
have been almost superhuman."

1545

Luís de Góis, a Portuguese, who later became a Jesuit, was
the first to take tobacco from America to Europe. Jean Ni-
cot, the French ambassador to the Court of Lisbon, later
sent a few leaves to France, where Catherine de Medici became addicted to the weed. The word "nicotine" comes
from the family name of the French diplomatic representative in Portugal.

When Ruy López de Villalobos, sailing from the west coast
of Mexico, explored New Guinea in 1545, his chief pilot was
the Portuguese Gonçalo Rico.

1549

March 29. The first Jesuits to reach the New World arrived
in Bahia, Brazil, with Tomé de Sousa, the first governor-

general. In the capital city of Portuguese America, the
Jesuits founded the first Jesuit college in the New World.
Portuguese Jesuits reached Japan in the same year.

1550   Gaspar Colaço, a Portuguese, was doing business in Potosí,
Upper Peru, now Bolivia.

By 1550, the town of Aveiro, Portugal, annually sent 150
ships to the fisheries of the Grand Banks.

1552   João Estaço, of the Order of the Hermits of St. Augustine,
a native of Angra, Terceira, Azores, was named bishop of
Puebla, Mexico. The Portuguese ecclesiastic entered religious life in 1520 and studied in his order's convent in sala-
manca, Spain, with St. Thomas of Villanova. After earning
the master's degree in theology, he left for Spanish America
as a missionary. In 1545 he became vicar provincial of the
Augustinians of Mexico. He died in the odor of sanctity on
April 4, 1553, before taking possession of his see.

1555   There are those who believe that João Caetano, a Portuguese
in the service of Spain, reached Hawaii in this year. The
official discovery, of 1778, is ascribed to Captain John Cook,
an Englishman.

1558   By this year, Henrique Garcês, a Portuguese born in Oporto,
had discovered mercury in Peru. Thanks to his discovery,
the production of silver in Potosí was greatly increased.
When he retired to Madrid, he published his Castilian translation of Os Lusíadas, the great Renaissance epic poem by
Luís de Camões, his fellow countryman. His was the third
such translation to appear in Spain.

1563   António Galvão, the Portuguese author, refers to Spanish
plans to build interocean canals on the isthmuses of Panamá
and Tehuántepec.

1565   A Portuguese by the name of Rodrigues Almeida discovered
a silver mine at Huantajaya, near Arica, on the Pacific
coast of South America.

1571   The Inquisition was formally established in New Spain in
1571, though it had been in operation since 1522. It was
finally abolished in 1820. During the sixteenth century, no
less than 43 Portuguese were sentenced by the Holy Office,
131 in the following century.

1572   Sir Francis Drake's voyage to Nombre de Diós, on the Gulf
              of Darién, was written up by Lopo or Lopes Vaz, a Portu-
              guese from Elvas. He also wrote the account of the voyage
              of John Oxnam of Plymouth to the West Indies and his jour-
              ney from Darién across the isthmus to the South Sea in 1575.
              This Portuguese chronicler, with "the discourse about him, "
              was taken at the Río de la Plata by the Earl of Cumberland
              in 1586.

              The epic poem, Os Lusíadas, by the Portuguese poet Luís
              de Camões, the outstanding poetic composition of the Re-
              naissance, appeared in Lisbon. It was translated for the
              first time by an American, the late Leonard Bacon, and
              published in 1950 by the Hispanic Society of America, New
              York, under the title of The Lusiads.
              Camões is inscribed on the Dartmouth Street façade of
              of the Boston Public Library near the ninth window.

1574   Gaspar Ferreira, a native of Oporto who made pantaloons
              in Guadalajara, New Spain, was condemned by the Inquisi-
              tion of the viceroyalty for being a "Lutheran heretic."

c. 1575   The Portuguese captain Alberto do Campo founded the town
              of Santiago del Saltillo, New Spain.

1577-1580   Sir Francis Drake, on his way around the world, took Nuno
              da Silva, a native of Oporto, Portugal, in the Cape Verde
              Islands. Silva was a pilot and got Drake to Brazil. Drake
              released him at Acapulco, on the west coast of New Spain.

1579   The first settler of the New Kingdom of León, viceroyalty
              of New Spain, was the Portuguese Luís de Carvalhal, or
              Luis de Carvajal y de la Cueva as he is known in Castilian,
              who was born in Mogodouro, Trás-os-Montes, Portugal, in
              1539 and raised in Benavente, Spain. An uncle, Duarte de
              Leão, sent him to the Cape Verde Islands, where he spent
              thirteen years before returning to Lisbon and eventually to
              Seville. In Seville he married Guiomar Álvares de Rivera,
              originally from Lisbon, a devout Jewess, the daughter of a
              Portuguese Jew who had served the Crown of Portugal as a
              slaver in Santo Domingo. Carvalhal arrived in Tampico,
              Mexico, in 1567 and returned to Spain in 1579. On March
              31, 1579, Philip II authorized him to discover, pacify, and
              settle a part of New Spain that would thenceforth be called
              the New Kingdom of León, an area of some 200,000 square
              miles that included part of Texas. On June 14 of the same

year Philip appointed him governor of the New Kingdom for life, with the right to name his successor. Some of Carvalhal's Jewish relatives in Spain sailed with him to the New World. The Portuguese-born conquistador arrived in Mexico City on November 12, 1580, and proceeded to Tampico, taking with him the settlers that he had brought from Spain. In 1581 or 1582 he founded a settlement on the site of the future Mexican city of Monterrey. About 1589, the Inquisition of Mexico City moved against him. Falsely accused of Judaism, he was sentenced in 1590 to an exile of six years from the Indies. He died in prison, the victim of his agony over the injustice of the trial. The first governor of the New Kingdom of León, the Portuguese Luís de Carvalhal, was the most prominent victim of the Mexican Inquisition.

1579   Until 1657, Antônio da Costa, a Portuguese, lived in Potosí, Upper Peru. He wrote a history of Potosí, the most important Portuguese treatise on Peru.

1580   With the death of Cardinal King Henry and the extinction of the House of Avis, Philip II of Castile made good his claim to the Portuguese throne -- his mother was an Avis -- by bribing important people and invading Portugal with an army under the Duke of Alba. Philip now became Philip I of Portugal, and he began the so-called Babylonian Captivity that lasted sixty years. In 1640 a revolution broke out in Lisbon, severed the dynastic connection, disarmed the Spanish garrisons, and restored the independence of the country under John IV, the first of the Bragança line. During the years 1580-1640 many Portuguese subjects of the Castilian Habsburgs moved virtually at will through Spanish lands, in Europe as in the New World and in the Philippines.

1583   The Portuguese captaincy of Newfoundland and the surrounding area, vested in the Corte-Real family, was extinguished.

While Sir Humfrey Gilbert was on St. John's to claim Newfoundland for England, the Portuguese fishermen he found there showered him with kindnesses "above those of other nations." In a note on the "liberalities of the Portingalls," he said that upon his departure they "put aboarde our provision, which was wines, bread or ruske, fish, wette and drie, sweet oyles, besides many other, as marmalades, figs, lymmons barrelled, and such like . . . . In brief, wee were supplied of our wants commodiously, as if we had been in countrey or some citie populous and plenty of all things."

1584   Simão Fernandes, a native of the Azores, piloted all the
              Elizabethan colonies to America. He was the master and
              pilot of Sir Walter Raleigh's expedition to Virginia in 1584.
              In 1585 he discovered Port Simon, Virginia. In 1587 Fer-
              nandes returned with John White to England.

1585   Nuevo Almadén, in the New Kingdom of León, viceroyalty
              of New Spain, was founded in this year, only to be abandoned
              shortly thereafter by Castanho de Sousa, a Portuguese, who
              left for New Mexico where he was arrested and eventually
              sent to the Moluccas.

1586-1588   Thomas Cavendish, following Drake's course, plundered
              Spanish commerce and circumnavigated the world. He cap-
              tured a Portuguese on the coast of Mexico by the name of
              Diogo. Farther north, on the California coast, Cavendish
              spied a Spanish ship and took "one Nicholas Roderigo a Por-
              tugall, who hath not only bene in Canton and other parts of
              China, but also in the island of Japon . . . and hath bene
              in the Philippinas."

1588   The Invincible Armada, which Philip II of Castile sent
              against England, sailed from Lisbon. Portugal supplied
              more ships and men to the undertaking than any other part
              of Philip's vast monarchy.

1589   Dom João da Gama, who had served as captain of the Portu-
              guese outpost of Malacca, sailed via Macau for Mexico
              across the Pacific. This is the first recorded voyage
              across the Pacific by a Portuguese ship.

              A Portuguese was identified as the governor of Cumaná,
              Venezuela.

1590   António Rodrigues de Leão Pinelo, ordinarily known by the
              Hispanicized form of his name, Antonio Rodríguez de León
              Pinelo, was the author of the first bibliography of the New
              World, Epítome de la Bibliografía oriental y occidental náu-
              tica y geográfica (Madrid, 1629). It is believed that he was
              born in Lisbon in 1590 or 1591. His grandfather was burned
              at the stake in Lisbon as a Judaizer in 1595. His father,
              Diogo Lopes, of Lisbon, moved to Buenos Aires in 1604,
              where later in life he became a Roman Catholic priest.
              Young Pinelo was educated in Spanish America, and pre-
              pared his famous bibliography, which is also filled with
              Portuguese references, in Lima, Peru. He spent his declin-

ing years in Spain, where he died in 1660 in the bosom of Holy Mother Church.

1593   A strong contingent of Portuguese soldiers arrived toward the end of the year in San Juan, Puerto Rico. The first garrison of the fortress of San Felipe del Morro was composed of Portuguese veterans, shipped from Lisbon by order of Philip II. Many of the men brought their wives, others married on the island. From these men descend the many Puerto Rican families with Portuguese patronymics.

The King of Cambodia sent two ambassadors to the Spanish governor of the Philippines. One was Diogo Veloso, a Portuguese.

1594   The Audiencia, or High Court, in Santo Domingo, declared that "more than half the people on the island are Portuguese."

March 21. Sebastião Rodrigues Sermenho, a Portuguese navigator in the service of Spain, sailed from Acapulco for Manila. He left Manila on the return voyage on July 5, 1595, with orders to explore the coast of the Pacific Northwest for the purpose of discovering a harbor to serve as a port of call for the Manila galleon whose regular run was between the Philippine capital and Acapulco. Seremenho sighted Cape Mendocino on November 4, 1595. On November 6, he cast anchor in Drake's Bay, which he named the Bay of San Francisco. On November 7, he formally took possession of the area for Spain. Continuing in a southerly direction, he reached the bay of San Luis Obispo at San Martin Island, and came to anchor in the port of Navidad, New Spain, on January 7, 1596. Later, the name Sermenho gave to Drake's Bay was transferred to the present bay and city of San Francisco.

1600   Pedro de Teixeira, a Portuguese navigator, reached the coast of California north of Cape Mendocino.

1602   Pedro Fernandes de Queirós, a Portuguese navigator in the service of Spain, brought to an end the great cycle of Portuguese-Spanish explorations. He sailed from Callao, Peru, crossed the Pacific, discovered Tahiti and the New Hebrides, and eventually returned to Mexico. Another Portuguese, Luís Vaz de Torres, who was part of the Queirós expedition, discovered Torres Straits (between Australia and New Guinea) in 1605.

1605   The Portuguese, according to the Spanish governor of Cuba,
            were said to "have shops and sell openly and in Seville they
            have correspondents of their nation. All the money is in
            their hands, gold and silver, which they send from here."
            It has been estimated that the Portuguese population of the
            Caribbean at this time amounted to between 10 and 15 per-
            cent of the total. This would account for the survival in the
            area, in Hispanicized form, of many Portuguese family
            names.

1606   May 14. Pedro Fernandes de Queirós, the Portuguese navi-
            gator mentioned under the year 1602, discovered and took
            possession of Australia for Spain, according to Carlos Sanz,
            the Spanish historian.

            In eight towns of Venezuela, including Caracas, there were
            115 Portuguese.

1607   In excavations in Jamestown, Virginia, the first permanent
            English settlement in America, sherds of Lisbon faience
            or majolica from the second half of the seventeenth century
            have been found.

1624   Luís Franco Rodrigues, a Portuguese New Christian born
            in Lisbon, was tried before the Inquisition of Cartagena,
            New Granada (Colombia). Two other Portuguese were in
            the auto-da-fé of the same Holy Office of March 24, 1638.

1630   Afonso de Benavides, a Portuguese Franciscan, published
            his famous Memorial in Madrid, a mission chronicle of
            New Mexico. Benavides was born in São Miguel, Azores,
            before 1579, the son of Pedro Afonso, scrivener of the cus-
            tomhouse of Ponta Delgada, and of Ana Murato de Benavides.
            He professed in the Franciscan convent of his native island
            or, according to other authors, in the Friary of St. Francis,
            Mexico City, in 1602. After serving in Cuernavaca and Te-
            manatla, he was appointed custos of the Franciscan mis-
            sions in New Mexico and commissary of the Holy Office for
            the same jurisdiction in October, 1623. He was formally re-
            ceived by the governor at Santa Fe on January 24, 1626. Up-
            on his return to Mexico City in the fall of 1629, he sailed for
            Spain where he presented his Memorial to Philip IV. In 1632
            he went to Rome as the confessor of Dom Francisco de Melo.
            In or about 1635, Benavides ended his activities at the Span-
          - ish Court and left for Lisbon where he became a member
            of the Portuguese Franciscan province and lived at the Fri-

ary of St. Francis. In 1639, having been made bishop-elect of Meliapor, India, he embarked for the Orient in the company of Dom Francisco dos Mártires, the Archbishop of Goa. He died en route to his post. Benavides' Memorial is a glowing tribute to the fertility and excellences of New Mexico, the New Kingdom of St. Francis.

1635 Matias de Sousa, a Portuguese, arrived in Maryland. One author wrote that he was "probably" of Jewish origin.

Simão Monteiro was born in Castelo Branco, Portugal. He lived in France and Italy and studied at one time to be a rabbi. He was brought before the Inquisition of Mexico and acquitted.

1636 The Portuguese of Lima, Peru, "having made themselves the masters of commerce, they almost wholly took over the so-called Street of Merchants . . . A Castilian who fails to enter a partnership with a Portuguese firm appears to have no prospect of success. They have cornered an entire mercantile fleet through credit they extend to one another. . . .they distribute merchandise through agents of their own own people throughout the kingdom [of Peru]."

1640 Of the sixty Portuguese in Potosí, Upper Peru, twenty were listed as being wealthy. One Antônio Afonso da Rocha Meneses had a fortune of 2,000,000 pesos. He was exiled for political reasons as the result of the restoration of Portugal on December 1.

1642 October 3. A Franciscan convent for men was founded in Puerto Rico by friars who had reached the island in 1641. Most of the friars were Portuguese. At the same time, many of the Dominicans on the island were also Portuguese.

1643 A Portuguese Catholic, married to a Dutch ensign, lived in New Amsterdam (Manhattan).

1648 October 8. The Marquess of Mancera, viceroy of Peru, wrote to the king of Spain from Lima: "As soon as the announcement reached this city of the treason of the Duke of Bragança, the uprising of Portugal, and the assurance that Brazil went along with it, quite apart from the great emotion and pain that it caused me, I became noticeably concerned because of the great number of Portuguese who live in these Kingdoms, and of the damage which might result

from any action which they might undertake, and with great
fear of those who were in the port of Buenos Aires, so near
as they are to Brazil, and stopping point on the way to this
Kingdom . . . ."

1654

Twenty-three Portuguese Jews from Recife, Brazil, arrived
in New Amsterdam following the collapse of Dutch power
in that part of South America on January 26. The Jews that
fled Pernambuco were at one time members of the Sephardic
community in Holland, having gone there originally from
Portugal to escape the Inquisition. When the Dutch West
India Company began its conquests in Brazil in 1630, Portuguese Jews from Holland soon found their way to America.
At the time of their defeat, the Dutch, wanting to protect
the Portuguese Jews who had been loyal to them, asked the
victorious Portuguese authorities to allow the Jews of Pernambuco to remain beyond the stipulated three-month period of grace until such time as the Dutch themselves, under
terms of the capitulations, wound up their own affairs, but
this was denied. Under the circumstances, the Jews considered it the better part of valor to leave at once, thus accounting for their arrival in New Amsterdam, which would
remain in Dutch control until 1664. These Portuguese Jewish refugees were the founders of the American Jewish community. The two oldest Jewish cemeteries in the country,
in Newport, Rhode Island, and in New York, have grave-
stones with Portuguese inscriptions, and the two historic
congregations used the Portuguese language until the second
half of the eighteenth century. In the course of time, other
Portuguese Jews settled in such places as Savannah, Charleston, and Philadelphia. The genealogies of American Jewry
are filled with ancient Portuguese names, e.g. Alvarez,
Azevedo, Cardozo, Carvalho, Castro, Costa, Crasto, Dias,
Duarte, Fernandes, Gomes, Henriques, Jorge, Lima, Lou-
zada, Lucena, Marques, Mendes, Mesquita, Miranda, Mon-
santo, Morais, Motta, Nunes, Pardo, Pacheco, Passos, Paz,
Pesoa, Peixotto, Pimenta, Pimentel, Pinheiro, Pinto, Portugal, Pretto, Sarzedas, Seixas, Silva, Silveira, Solis, Souza,
Touro, and Valverde.

1658

The Masonic Order was introduced in the Thirteen Colonies
by the fifteen Jewish families of Spanish-Portuguese stock
who arrived in Newport, Rhode Island.

1662-1685

An oil painting, of unknown origin, of Catherine of Bragança,
the Portuguese consort of Charles II of Great Britain, hangs

in its original frame in the Ballroom, Governor's Palace, Williamsburg, Virginia. In New York City, Queens Borough and Queens College perpetuate the memory of the Portuguese queen.

1672   A Portuguese Franciscan, Gonçalo da Madre de Deus, born Gonçalo de Meneses e Lencastre, who fled his native land for political reasons, was responsible for the rebuilding of the new city of Panamá after Henry Morgan, the English pirate, captured and burned Old Panamá in 1671. Friar Gonçalo found his way to Spanish America from Castile. He worked for a while in the mines of Mexico, then moved to Guatemala where he entered religion. He arrived in Old Panamá in 1669, prepared to convert the "wicked" city to Christian living. When his efforts proved unavailing, he left for Peru to raise enough money to build a new city that would be destined for the Elect of God. In 1672, back in Panamá with helpers and money, he began the construction of his city of virtue, but all in vain. In the following year it became the capital of Panamá. Gonçalo himself was arrested for the crime of being a Portuguese and returned to Spain as a prisoner.

1677   A group of Portuguese Jews from Barbados settled in Newport, Rhode Island. Other settlers later came from Curaçao, The Netherlands, Brazil, and Portugal.

1695   Sister Juana Inés de la Cruz (born 1651), the celebrated Mexican poet who has been called the "Tenth Muse" and the "American Phoenix, " died in Mexico City. Among her prose works was a theological reply to one of the writings of the celebrated Portuguese Jesuit, António Vieira (1608-1697), the master of sacred eloquence who has been called the Portuguese Chrysostom, and whose checkered and brilliant career included service as chaplain to Queen Christina of Sweden in Rome. Vieira had an enormous impact in Spain and Spanish America.

1700   Plays on the canonization of the Portuguese St. John of God were staged in Mexico City. St. John of God was born in Portugal in 1495 and died in Spain in 1550.

1700-1770   Madeira was a good market for Pennsylvania grain and New England cod and in turn Madeira was the principal source of the wine drunk in the Thirteen Colonies and in the West Indies. The Madeira of the eighteenth century, which George

Washington and Thomas Jefferson served, was a heady table wine, not the noble generous wine of today.

1727-76   In Pennsylvania, the oath of allegiance to the British crown was administered to a number of Germans, Dutch, French, Swiss, and Portuguese.

1730   Isaac Mendes Seixas, a Portuguese Jew, arrived in New York from Portugal. His son, Benjamin Mendes Seixas, of New York and Newport, was one of the founders of the New York Stock Exchange.

1731   Aaron Lopes, baptized as a Catholic with the name of Duarte and also known as Aires, was born in Lisbon. He married Ana, a relative, again in the Catholic Church. His brother Moses fled Portugal in the early 1740s but Duarte did not get to Newport, Rhodes Island, until 1752. Here he openly professed Judaism and changed his name to Aaron. He became "one of the wealthiest merchants and shipppers" of his day, built up the whaling industry, and owned at one time about thirty ships, assertedly manned by Azorean seamen. This most famous of eighteenth century Portuguese-American Jews died in 1782.

1732   A group of Spanish-Portuguese Jews settled in Savannah in the very year that Oglethorpe began the colonization of Georgia. They came from England, which since 1655 had permitted the reentry of Jews.

1734   David Mendes Machado, a native of Lisbon, became the rabbi of the Spanish-Portuguese Congregation Searith Israel of New York City.

1737   Abraham de Lyon (Leão?), who was a vintner in Portugal before coming to the United States, began the growing of grapes in Georgia.

c. 1750   According to the records of Robeson County, South Carolina, shipwrecked Portuguese sailors landed near Georgetown, South Carolina, and gradually intermarried with Indians and Negroes. The claim of those who say they descend from these people is clothed in mystery.

1752   The first Azorean families reached Porto de Viamão. They were the founders of the bustling and progressive city of Porto Alegre, capital of the Brazilian state of Rio Grande do

Sul. An impressive monument to these Azorean pioneers
has recently been inaugurated in Porto Alegre, and the public area where it stands is known as the Park of the Azoreans. This is the grandest tribute ever paid to the Azorean
people.

1755   Following the Lisbon earthquake of November 1, 1755, a
                group of Portuguese Jews is said to have sailed from Portu-
                gal to Virginia. Bad winds apparently forced the passengers
                to seek refuge in Narragansett Bay and they settled in New-
                port.

1760   The Portuguese table on display in Decatur House, the head-
                quarters of the National Trust for Historic Preservation,
                Washington, D.C., was probably built between 1760 and
                1775.

                There is a Portuguese altar door, c. 1765, and an oratório
                or portable altar, c. 1760, also of Portuguese construction,
                in a small chapel in the sanctuary of the Samuel S. Fleisher
                Art Memorial, administered by the Philadelphia Museum
                of Art. The piece were selected by Dr. Robert C. Smith,
                the distinguished art historian of the University of Pennsyl-
                vania who died on August 20, 1975.

1761   The General Assembly of Rhode Island authorized James
                Lucena to manufacture Castile soap, who thus began the
                industry in the United States. Lucena, who got the formula
                from Portugal, became a citizen in the same year.

1763   December 2. The Touro Synagogue of Newport, Rhode Is-
                land, the oldest extant synagogue in the United States, was
                dedicated. Among the founders was Aaron Lopes, a native
                of Lisbon.

1765   The Nantucket whalers extended their operations to the
                Azores. During the next two centuries, men from the
                Azores were employed on whaleships throughout the world.
                William Pitt is quoted as having said in 1785 that "the Portu-
                guese had now . . . a very pretty spermaceti whale fishery,
                which they had learned from the New Englanders, and car-
                ried on upon the coast of Brazil."

c. 1770   José Dias, a Portuguese, settled on Martha's Vineyard. He
                married a local woman, was converted to his wife's Baptist

faith, and served in the American Revolutionary War. Captured by the British, he died in their custody in 1781.

1776   In his Wealth of Nations, Adam Smith had this to say about Madeira wine. "Madeira wine, not being a European commodity, could be imported directly into America and the West Indies, countries which, in all their nonenumerated commodities, enjoyed a free trade to the island of Madeira. These circumstances had probably introduced that general taste for Madeira wine, which our officers found established in all our colonies at the commencement of the war that began in 1755, and which they brought back with them to the mother-country, where that wine had not been much in fashion before."

1779   September 23. The first American warship, Bonne Homme Richard, under the command of John Paul Jones, a native of Scotland, engaged the Serapis, a frigate of the English navy, and captured her "near the coast of Great Britain, and in view, by moonlight, of numerous spectators." Of the 201 men on board, only 78 were Americans. The others were distributed among the following nationalities: English, 54; Portuguese, 28; Irish, 19; Swedish, 7; Scottish, 5; Norwegian, 3; French, 3; and miscellaneous, 4. Three Portuguese seamen were killed.

1780   Men from the Azorean islands of Faial, Pico, São Jorge, Flores, and Corvo embarked as members of the crews of 200 whalers which later took them to the United States.

1789   Between this year and 1815, it is presumed that the Portuguese founded whaling stations along the California coast at Half Moon Bay, Pescadero, Monterey, Carmel, San Simeon, Point Conception, Portuguese Cove, Portuguese Bend, and San Diego.

1790   Salvador Fidalgo, a Portuguese navigator, discovered a stretch of the Pacific coast south of Alaska.

In the first United States census, the following residents with Portuguese or quasi-Portuguese names were reported from New York City and County: Benjamin Seixias, Rachel Pinto, Gershom Seixias, Rebecca Gomez, Isaac Gomez, Jr., Francis Silver, Isaac M. Gomez, Mary Farrara, Isaac Navarro, Joseph Pinto, Joseph Silve, Isaac Montanye, Jr., John Montanye, and David Navarro. From Charleston District,

South Carolina: Samuel De Costa, Aaron Lopus, and Sarah
De Costa. No obviously Portuguese names are listed in
Newport town, Rhode Island; in Providence Town, only John
Gonsolve. There were no Portuguese heads of families in
New Bedford and Sherburn Town, Nantucket County, Massa-
chusetts. And none in Brooklyn Town. In Philadelphia,
there were two Portuguese-surnamed heads of families:
Peter Facundus, a shoemaker, and John Telles, a merchant.
In Williamsburg, Virginia, an Elizabeth Rozario was listed
among the free people.

c. 1790   The two chandeliers hanging in the Cross Hall on the State
Floor of the White House were made in England in the Adam
style for the Lisbon residence of the Counts of Porto Covo.
When the Porto Covo Palace was purchased by the British
government for use as its embassy, the chandeliers were
sold to a dealer in New York. They were given to the White
House in 1946 by an anonymous donor.

The four crystal wall sconces in the John Quincy Adams
State Drawing Room, Department of State, are from the
same period. They were removed from the Porto Covo Palace of Lisbon in 1953.

1792   Two Portuguese deserted from the ship commanded by
George Vancouver when it put in at Monterey, California.

1794   When he sailed from Hawaii, George Vancouver, the English
explorer, reported leaving behind a Portuguese.

1803   Some Portuguese had settled in New Orleans even before
the Louisiana Purchase of this year. Others reached Louisiana as members of the crew of Jean Lafitte, the French
pirate who helped the Americans.

1809   Moses Seixas, a Portuguese Jew, died. On his tombstone,
in the Old Synagogue, Newport, Rhode Island, was this inscription: "He was Grand Master of the Grand Lodge of the
Masonic order of this State & Cashier of the Bank of Rhode
Island from its commencement to his death."

1812   There are three Portuguese names on the master roll of
American ships in the Battle of Lake Erie. One of these
sailors, known as "Portuguese Joe," became a hero of the
Great Lakes engagements. He died in New Orleans about
the middle of the century.

1814   A number of Portuguese took part in the Battle of New Or-
              leans and in other fighting in this area.

1815   The first recorded Portuguese settler in California was An-
              tónio José Rocha, who deserted from the schooner Columbia
              at Monterey. In 1816, José Maria Rocha, a Portuguese,
              was working for relatives in Los Angeles. In 1828, José
              António was granted the 4,600 La Brea Rancho. He built a
              house in what is now Culver City, the famous mill at Mis-
              sion San Gabriel, and the adobe structure which in 1853 be-
              came the Los Angeles City Hall. He is also credited with
              establishing some of the earliest whaling stations in Cali-
              fornia. António José Rocha became a Mexican citizen in
              1831. In 1836 he lived in Santa Barbara with his wife and
              five children. A son, António José Rocha, served as the
              district judge of Balboa, 1868-1873. The last descendant
              of the pioneer Angeleno was António Ricardo Rocha, born
              in 1866, who died without issue in January, 1938.

1816   John Eliot de Castro, possibly a Portuguese, served as the
              secretary to the king of Hawaii.

              The Rev. Peter Babad (1763-1846), a member of the Society
              of St. Sulpice of Baltimore and a native of France, taught
              Portuguese for the first time in an American institution of
              higher learning, St. Mary's College, Baltimore.

1816-1818   Dr. Fernandes, a friend and correspondent of Thomas Jef-
              ferson of Norfolk, Virginia, was the only physician in
              America that the Abbé José Correia da Serra trusted.

1820   The Rev. Peter Babad, the French Sulpician who taught at
              St. Mary's College, Baltimore, published A Portuguese and
              English Grammar, compiled from those of Lobato, Durham,
              Sane and Vieyra, and simplified for the Use of Students (Bal-
              timore: Fielding Lucas). This was the first grammar of
              the Portuguese language published in the United States and
              it was dedicated to the Abbé José Correia da Serra, the Por-
              tuguese minister. Before his time, Americans wishing to
              learn Portuguese probably used the grammar published in
              London in 1768 by Anthony Vieyra.

1826   April 15. Jacinto Pereira, known as Jason Perry, was born
              in Faial, Azores. The proprietor of a dry goods store in
              Honolulu, he was one of the most distinguished among the
              early Portuguese in Hawaii. He served as a consular agent

and was instrumental in getting the Hawaiian authorities to
recruit laborers from Madeira to come to Hawaii for contract work. Later, Portuguese labor immigrants also came
from the Azores and Portugal proper. Perry died in Hawaii
on March 27, 1883.

c. 1830   Commercial intercourse between New Bedford, Massachu-
            setts, and the Azores dates from this time. The emigration
            of people also began at about the same time.

            The first Portuguese who arrived in substantial numbers in
            New England came on the whalers sent out from New Bed-
            ford, the most important whaling port of the East.

1830-1879   There were about 400 Cape Verdeans and Azoreans, deser-
            ters from their whaling ships, in the Hawaiian Islands.

1831   Pietro Bachi, an exiled Sicilian who taught Portuguese at
            Harvard College, 1826-1846, published his grammar of the
            Portuguese language, the second such work to appear in the
            United States.

c. 1840   Several hundred Portuguese, for the most part unmarried,
            were recruited from the Azores as contract laborers by the
            Louisiana sugar plantations. Many of these immigrants
            married creole women and apparently remained on the plan-
            tations until the Civil War. In 1847 they founded the first
            Portuguese mutual aid society in the United States, the
            Lusitanian-Portuguese Benevolent Association, which still
            exists in New Orleans. After the Civil War, most of the
            settlers left for California and some seem to have returned
            to Portugal.

1849   There appeared in Oporto, Portugal, a booklet of eighteen
            pages, in Portuguese, on California and the Gold Rush,
            whose title in English dress reads as follows: News and
            announcements of mercantile interest, extracted from offi-
            cial documents, on California and its gold mines. Contain-
            ing: general considerations -- history and geography, ap-
            pearance of the country, fertility of the land, and its cli-
            mate -- character and customs of its inhabitants -- gold
            mines -- silver, platinum, mercury, and pearls -- ways
            to go to California -- the means of acquiring the gold with-
            out going there - merchandise that properly may be shipped
            to California, and their prices -- &t. &t. The description
            of California is golden. "A country teeming with gold and

precious metals necessarily attracts a great multitude of people, as indeed we see. Moreover this country has an excellent climate, a soil of incomparable fertility, and occupies a geographical position well suited for it to become the Universal Emporium of the Trade of Asia and Europe. These innumerable throngs of people who are flocking into California from every quarter of the globe are entirely employed in the exploitation of gold, they lack even the most indispensable comforts of life although they have plenty of gold to buy them. So long as these mines continue to produce gold in such abundance people will not apply themselves to any other labor, and for this reason that country will be for many years the best market for European products."

A number of Azoreans, and possibly other Portuguese from Portugal proper, took part in the Gold Rush to California, leading to an increase in the Portuguese population of the area. In 1850, there were 109 Portuguese in California; in 1860, 1,560.

1850

The migration of Portuguese to Mendocino and Fort Bragg, California, began. They were employed in the mines and lumber mills. In 1870, António Luís, a native of Terceira, Azores, established Lisbon House on Ukiah Street, Fort Bragg, a famous landmark for many years.

The 'fore-the-mast immigration from the Azores and the Cape Verde Islands was in full swing, and many thousands from the Atlantic islands came in this way to the United States. Unlike the incoming masses from other lands, the Portuguese generally worked their way across the Atlantic as whalemen on ships of New Bedford, Nantucket, and other whaling ports.

António Vitorino was in charge of the building in Monterey, California, which served as the Portuguese whaling station.

1850-1860

During this decade there were Portuguese settlers in old Mission San Jose, California. The Mission was dedicated by Father Fermín Lasuén, June 11, 1797.

"In the fifties many went to California, joining the gold rush. In order to get there, hundreds signed on with New Bedford whaleships, which were then working in the Arctic from bases in Alaska -- sailing eighteen thousand miles around Cape Horn and up the west coast, through the Bering Straits

and on to Point Barrow, Herschel Island, and other points
on the Alaskan coast, near the newly discovered bowhead
whaling grounds. "

Over 800 Portuguese miners migrated to California in
search of gold. (In 1860 there were 844 Portuguese miners
in the state.) The only Portuguese-dominated mining settlement was at Hawkinsville, Yreka township, Siskiyou
County. It continued to exist during the second half of the
nineteenth century.

California shore whaling, in which the Portuguese played
an important role, began in Monterey in the 1850s, reached
its peak in the 1860s and 1870s, and disappeared in the
1880s. At one time there were eighteen whaling stations in
California, i.e. Crescent City, Bolinas Bay, Half Moon Bay,
Pescadero, Santa Cruz, Monterey, Carmel, Point Sur, San
Simeon, Avila, Point Conception, Goleta, Portuguese Bend,
San Pedro, and San Diego.

1851   Whaling in Monterey, California, began in this year. The
            Monterey Whaling Company came into being in 1854; it was
            reorganized in 1855 with seventeen Portuguese seamen and
            two boats. A new company was organized in 1858, and in
            1873 the two companies merged, bringing together twenty-
            three whalemen.

            Manuel F. Cabral, from Ribeiras, Pico, Azores, arrived
            in Point Loma on San Diego bay, California. August Mark
            Vaz believes that he was the earliest Portuguese pioneer.
            Francisco G. Simas, from the same place of origin, ar-
            rived in 1861. Manuel Ávila was in Point Loma in 1874 but
            died in Chile, in 1884. A few Azoreans stayed in Chile and
            encouraged members of their family to join them. One such
            person, a native of Corvo, was the well-known and respec-
            ted Nascimento Jorge, who served at one time as consul of
            Portugal and in 1963 owned and operated the great publishing
            house of Nascimento, in Santiago.

            Five Portuguese took the oath of allegiance to the kingdom
            of Hawaii. Before 1850, 37 Portuguese nationals became
            naturalized Hawaiians, the third largest Western group (af-
            ter the United States and Great Britain). In 1850, out of a
            class of 109, 10 were Portuguese. In 1852, 4 were natural-
            ized from the Azores, 1 from Portugal.

c. 1852   José Machado, an Azorean who became known as Joseph
               Clark, arrived in California. In 1858 he worked on a whaler
               based in San Diego. Like most of the sixty whalers that
               fished off the coast of Lower California, the crews were
               generally made up of Portuguese. In 1864, Clark was oper-
               ating at Portuguese Bend, near San Pedro.

1853   Captain António Mendes, said to have been the first person
               to navigate the Sacramento River, California, arrived in
               San Francisco. He was born in Terceira, Azores, and
               joined the crew of a whaling expedition bound for the China
               Sea. Once in California, he tried his hand at mining. In
               time he bought several ships and plied them between Stock-
               ton and Sacramento, then between Sacramento and San Fran-
               cisco. In later life he farmed in Sutter County.

1855   A native of the Azores, with a corrupted Portuguese name,
               Antone S. Sylvia arrived in New Bedford, Massachusetts,
               at the age of fifteen aboard the Silver Cloud, later outfitted
               as a whaler. Sylvia, who died in 1920, became a millionaire.
               He began as a clerk in the Joseph Frazer Whaling Outfitting
               Company, New Bedford, and in 1862 became the sole propri-
               etor of the business, expanding it until it was the outstand-
               ing store of its kind.

               One of the earliest Portuguese pioneers of the Sacramento,
               California, area was Tionio (António?) da Rosa, known as
               Tionio Waters, who came from Faial, Azores, about 1855.
               Two other Azoreans, from São Jorge, Manuel Bento and José
               de Sousa, came in 1860-1861.

1856   The first Portuguese family from the Azores to settle in
               Fall River, Massachusetts, was that of Mrs. Maria de Jesus
               Cunha, also known as Wager, who brought a number of sons
               and daughters with her, including a daughter with the Angli-
               cized name of Emeline Elizabeth Perry.

1856-1857   Fourteen Portuguese from the Azores and two from Portugal
               became citizens of Hawaii. In 1858-59, thirty from the
               Azores, six from the Cape Verde Islands. In 1860-61,
               twenty-one from the Azores, six from the Cape Verdes.

1858   The San Leandro Gazette, the only newspaper in Alameda
               County, California, complained about landlords who deman-
               ded exorbitant rents. ". . . the Portuguese had gone on
               renting, and from renting buying, until many of them are
               now well of and all of them making something."

1859 — William Taylor had this to say about whaling: "Fisheries are becoming a fruitful product of the California coast! A company of Portuguese in Monterey have gone into the whale fishery along the coast, and have taken from whales which they have captured since March, 1856, say eight months, sixteen thousand gallons of oil, which were sold for twelve thousand dollars."

1860-1880 — According to the manuscript Census of Population, California, there were 1,717 persons of Portuguese foreign stock in the state in 1860; 13,159, in 1880. Of the latter, 7,990 were foreign-born.

1861 — António S. Silva, a pioneer settler of San Leandro, California, bought land north of San Leandro Creek. His descendants have borne the names of Carvalho and Oakes. ("Carvalho" means "oak" in Portuguese.) Oakes Boulevard perpetuates the family name.

José António, a cabinetmaker, native of Portugal, worked in Philadelphia before the Civil War. None of his furniture has been identified.

1862 — There are two Portuguese names on the Massachusetts Honor Roll of men who died for the Union in the Civil War: Elisha N. Ávila, killed at Fort Donaldson, February 14; and Antone Frates (Freitas), killed in action on June 2.

The whaling station at Carmel, California, was founded by Azoreans and Madeirans from Monterey.

1864 — A passport was issued at Horta, Faial, Azores, to Maria Loriana Cunha (c. 1830-1887), said to have been the first Portuguese woman to land in Hawaii.

1866 — In this year, according to Leo Pap, "when the end of the Civil War enabled the Federal Government to take a stronger stand again against the Plains Indian tribes, the northwestern part of the United States also acquired its Portuguese hero -- even though there has never been any sizable Portuguese settlement in that region. A fort being built along the Bozeman Trail, in the State of Wyoming, was suddnely threatened with extinction by a savage Indian attack. A volunteer was needed to break through the siege lines and call for help at the next fort. This meant riding some 240 miles through hostile territory, in freezing snow. John Phillipe,

a woodchopper employed at the embattled new fort and known
there simply as 'Portuguese John', undertook the almost im-
possible task -- which has been called a much greater feat
than the famous ride of Paul Revere during the Revolution.
Born as João or Manuel Felipe in the western Azores, Phillipe had settled in California after the Gold Rush, but later
drifted into Wyoming, where he died in 1883."

1868   The first Portuguese in Portsmouth, Rhode Island, arrived
in this year.

August 6. A group of Portuguese immigrants in San Francisco founded the Portuguese Protective and Benevolent Association of the City and County of San Francisco, also
known as the Associação Portuguesa Protectora e Beneficente
do Estado da Califórnia or by its initials A.P.P.B., the first
Portuguese organization of its kind in California. The first
president of this fraternal and mutual aid society was Dr.
Henrique Rocha Martinho, a San Francisco dentist born in
Madeira who changed his name to Henry Morton. By 1872
the A.P.P.B. had five "halls," in San Francisco, San Leandro, Sacramento, Sonoma, and Centerville, all under the
"Grand Council" of San Francisco. It was incorporated under the laws of the state of California at least as early as
January 29, 1875. In 1877, Dr. José de Sousa Bettencourt,
a prominent Portuguese physician of San Francisco, joined
the society. He was elected president in 1884. Under his
leadership, the society played a role in local affairs. During the years 1890-1910, the activities of the association
were limited to San Francisco and environs. Following the
earthquake of 1906, and under the aegis of António Martinho
Carvalho, a prominent Portuguese of San Francisco, the
association expanded its activities. Between 1911 and 1921,
nine affiliates were organized in a number of California cities and towns. In 1922, the affairs of the now enlarged association were centralized in a "Supreme Council." By 1933
the society had 2,200 members in fifty-two affiliates. It was
already beginning to feel the impact of Manuel Reis, who became an officer in 1930. In 1938 the society was granted
a state license as a fraternal insurer. By 1947 a total of
eighty-four affiliates, now known as "councils," were in operation. Earlier, in 1945, women were admitted to membership for the first time. In the same year, following his
discharge from the army, Jack Costa returned to his old job
as head of the accounting department. He has been actively
involved with the affairs of the society ever since. In 1948,

the corporate name was changed to "Benevolent Society of California, " to reflect the society's broader, less ethnic appeal. On July 1, 1957 the successor of the A.P.P.B. merged with the União Portuguesa Continental (Portuguese Continental Union) to form the United National Life Insurance Society. The fraternal, social, and cultural activities of United National were now taken over by its new division, the Luso-American Fraternal Federation. A second division, the Luso-American Educational Foundation, was created on July 12, 1963, to promote the educational and cultural development of the Portuguese people.

1869   Before this year, some 800 Portuguese Catholics worshipped at St. Mary's Church, the first Roman Catholic Church of New Bedford, Massachusetts. In 1867, Father Nóia, a priest from the Azores, arrived on the scene but death cut short his ministry. In 1869 Father João Inácio Azevedo became the pastor of the Portuguese community. It was he who founded the new parish of St. John the Baptist. When St. John's was canonically instituted on September 10, 1871, it became the second Roman Catholic parish of New Bedford. The cornerstone for the first St. John's was laid on September 27, 1874, and the church was dedicated on June 27. 1875. The second pastor of the Portuguese parish was the Rev. António de Mattos Freitas, a native of Calheta, São Jorge, Azores, who retired because of ill health and returned to his native land. He was succeeded by the Rev. António G. da Silva Neves, who served as pastor for twenty-five years, until ill health in turn forced him to retire. It was during his pastorate that the new and larger Church of St. John the Baptist began to be built at County and Wing streets, where it still stands. "The magnificent Church of St. John the Baptist is a land mark in New Bedford, befitting its position as mother church of the Portuguese in the United States."

A prominent Portuguese whaleman with an Anglicized name, Captain Joe Clark, built the wharf at San Simeon, California. The names Portuguese Flats and Portuguese Lane remain as reminders of the pioneers. In 1960 the Portuguese whaling station at San Simeon was formally declared a California State Historical Monument (No. 726).

1870   The Portuguese in California began to turn more and more to to dairying, a calling in which they are still preeminent.

The U.S. Census of 1870 lists the number of Portuguese-born

residents at 4,542. Of these, 2,508 were in California; 104, in Nevada; 735, in Massachusetts; 237, in New York; 125, in Louisiana; and 76, in Illinois. According to the same source, 2,658 Portuguese entered the United States in 1861-1870.

May 24. Associate Justice Benjamin Nathan Cardozo, of the United States Supreme Court, a Portuguese-surnamed descendant of pre-Revolutionary Sephardic stock, was born in New York City. The eminent jurist graduated from Columbia College in 1889 and was admitted to the Bar in 1891. In 1913 he was elected to the Supreme Court of New York. In the same year he became an associate judge pro tempore of the Court of Appeals, an appointment that was regularized in 1917. In 1926 he was elected chief judge of the same court. His court became the second most distinguished tribunal in the land. A man of learned bents, Cardozo wrote, among other works, The Nature of the Judicial Process (1921), a classic of its kind. In 1932 he was named to the Supreme Court of the United States and served on the high bench until his death on July 9, 1938.

Manuel Sylvia, a native of São Jorge, Azores, first settled in Troy, New York. He moved to Little Compton, Rhode Island in the 1870s. He is recognized as the earliest Portuguese settler in the Rhode Island community. Many of the pioneer Portuguese immigrants to New England with the names of Silva or Silveira Anglicized them to Sylvia.

By the decade of the 1870s, the Portuguese settlers of San Leandro, California were already observing the festival of Pentecost in the typical way that has characterized the Portuguese and Portuguese-Americans of California to this day. There is a reference to the Festival of the Holy Ghost (Festa do Espírito Santo) in William Halley, The Centennial Year Book of Alameda County (Oakland, 1876), where Portuguese names appear truncated and mangled almost beyond recognition.

1871   January 5. Chief Justice António J. Perry, of the Hawaiian Supreme Court, was born in Honolulu, the son of Jason and Anna (Henriques) Perry, both of Faial, Azores. President Calvin Coolidge nominated him as chief justice of the Supreme Court on February 18, 1926. He was reappointed in 1930.

1872   February 18. Jacinth M. de Gouveia was born in São Miguel,
            Azores. He arrived in Hawaii in 1880 and died in Honolulu
            on June 12, 1956. He is said to have introduced linguiça,
            the savory Portuguese smoked pork sausage into the islands.
            The Portuguese words for three different kinds of Portuguese
            sausages, linguiça, chouriço, and morcela continue to be
            generally understood.

1874   March 10. The Rev. António de Mattos Freitas, a native
            of Sao Jorge, Azores, began the first Portuguese parish of
            Fall River, Massachusetts, as a mission. On June 25, 1892,
            the mission became a parish under the invocation of Senhor
            Santo Cristo dos Milagres (Lord Holy Christ of the Miracles),
            a devotion very dear to the people of São Miguel, Azores.
            The new church structure was finally dedicated in 1942,
            with the presence of Dom Manuel Salgueiro, Archbishop of
            Évora, Portugal. The Portuguese Catholic parishes of Fall
            River also include: St. Michael the Archangel, a mission
            in 1896, a parish in 1902; Espírito Santo, a mission in 1904,
            in its own church in 1910; St. Anthony of Padua, 1911; St.
            Elizabeth, first a mission, then a parish in 1915; Our Lady
            of the Angels, September 6, 1915; and Our Lady of Health,
            1924.

            May 31. The Portuguese Society of the Most Blessed Trin-
            ity (Sociedade Portuguesa da Santíssima Trindade) was
            founded in Erie, Pennsylvania, by twenty-five Azoreans
            who had been contracted to work in the factories. Later
            the society established a branch in Rochester, New York,
            which declared its independence in the 1930s under the name
            of Rochester Portuguese American Association. The Erie
            society published the first Portuguese-language newspaper
            on the East Coast. The revised statutes of the Erie society,
            approved on September 2, 1951, limited membership to Ro-
            man Catholics who were Portuguese or descendants of Por-
            tuguese. The Erie society also has the distinction of being
            the oldest Portuguese society established on the East Coast.

1875   April 11. Antone Ferreira Tavares was born in the Azores.
            He was admitted to the Bar of Hawaii in 1898. At the time
            of his retirement in February, 1926, he was also a suc-
            cessful business man. He was elected to the Territorial
            House of Representatives in 1911 and reelected for five con-
            secutive terms. In 1920 he was elected to the Territorial
            Senate and reelected for a four-year term.

There were over 400 Portuguese living in Hawaii, many of them former seamen from whaling vessels.

1876

The Azores Band marched in the parade commemorating the centennial of the founding of New Bedford, Massachusetts.

The Guillermo Castro Ranch of Hayward, California, was partitioned in this year. A number of Portuguese settlers bought parcels of land, among them João Vieira Goulart, a native of São João, Pico, Azores, whose 306 acres were beyond the Fairview district. Goulart worked as a whaleman on a whaler based in New England, and sailed to New Zealand and the Antarctic. He brought his family from the Azores after the Civil War, reaching San Francisco in 1869, on a voyage that took them from the Azores to Brazil, Argentina, around Cape Horn to Chile, and then up the coast to California. During the Klondike gold rush of 1898, Goulart and his two sons went to Alaska. This pioneer Portuguese died in 1910 at the age of 83.

Joseph Manta, described as a "venturesome shipowner," was the mogul of the Provincetown, Massachusetts, Portuguese fleet.

The Hawaiian Gazette of Honolulu said, following the action of the Board of Immigration, November 6, to defray the cost of bringing 200 persons from the Portuguese North Atlantic islands, that there were already "about 400 Portuguese here," adding that they were "among the most industrious of our people. . . ."

1877

The Sociedade Portuguesa de Santo António Beneficente de Hawaii (Portuguese Benevolent Society of St. Anthony of Hawaii) was founded. It celebrated its fiftieth anniversary in 1927 with the publication of a bi-lingual history of the organization, Jubilee of St. Antonio Society (1877-1927) Jubileu da Sociedade Portuguesa de Santo Antonio Beneficente de Hawaii.

Of the forty-eight captains commanding Grand Bankers out of Provincetown, Massachusetts, six were Yankees, thirty-three were Nova Scotians, and nine were Portuguese.

The Jornal de Notícias, the first Portuguese newspaper published in the United States, appeared in or about 1877.

1878

September 29. The Priscilla, a German bark, landed the

first Portuguese immigrants in Honolulu. The group of Madeirans numberd 120 persons (60 men, 22 women, and 38 children), the pioneers of the present-day Portuguese community. The Priscilla is the Mayflower of the Portuguese of Hawaii.

The mass migration of Portuguese to the Hawaiian Islands began in 1878 and continued until 1899. By this time 12,780 had come. By 1910, more than 21,000 had arrived.

1879   José (Joe) Pimentel and his brothers, Portuguese immigrants, are listed in the Hayward, California, directory as owning five acres of farm land adjacent to the present-day Catholic Church in the Second and E streets area. In the early 1850s, Joe, a Forty-Niner, opened a barber shop, with hot baths and a massage parlor, in Hayward, which became a popular meeting place for local politicians and others. He was instrumental in organizing the Hayward branch of the Portuguese Benevolent Society of San Francisco. When Hayward was incorporated as a city in 1876, Joseph Pimentel was elected to the first Board of City Trustees and named clerk. In 1877 the board gave Pimentel a twenty-year concession to lay water mains in the community. From 1896 until his death in 1903 he served as justice of the peace of Eden Township. In 1911, Charles Pimentel, his son, was deputy recorder of Alameda County and ran his father's barber shop at the same time.

1880   According to the U.S. Census of 1880, there were 7,512 natives of the Portuguese Atlantic islands in the country, 8,138 from Portugal proper. California reported 3,356 from the islands, 4,705 from the continent; Massachusetts, 2,421 and 1,161; and Rhode Island, 185 and 210. (The census takers were obviously not aware of the Portuguese reality, and mistook an extraordinary number of islanders for continentals.)

The Brotherhood of the Holy Ghost of the Holy Trinity was founded in Hawaii by the Portuguese community. The Brotherhood was organized to celebrate the religious holidays of the liturgical year, such as Christmas and the seven days after Easter Sunday (in the traditional Portuguese Church, the seven Domingas).

August 1. Thirty Portuguese men, all but one from the Azores, met in San Leandro, California (then a city of 878

inhabitants and until the earthquake of 1868 the seat of Alameda County) to found Council No. 1 of the União Portuguesa
do Estado da Califórnia (Portuguese Union of the State of
California), generally known by its initials U. P. E. C., one
of the largest and most prestigious Portuguese beneficent
associations in the United States. The origins of the society
are not clear, but Council No. 1 seems to have been the successor of the Portuguese Brotherhood of the State of California, organized as early as 1876. The guiding spirit of the
U. P. E. C. during its early days was António Fonte, the first
president of the San Leandro Council and the first supreme
president of the Supreme Council when the latter was formed
in 1887. He relinquished the high office in 1893, and thereafter served the society as a director until his death on
April 7, 1906. By October 3, 1887, when the first annual
convention was held, the U. P. E. C. had grown to four councils, in San Leandro, Hollister, Hayward, and Petaluma.
At the beginning, whenever a member died, each living
member gave $1.00 to the widow and children. This simple
system of mutual aid gave way in 1892 to regular insurance
coverage. In 1889, the San Leandro Council built its own
assembly hall. Here were housed the offices of the Supreme
Council until 1909, when it moved into its own building. In
1964, the Supreme Council and Council No. 1, at a cost of
about $225,000, built their present joint headquarters, the
impressive U. P. E. C. Cultural Center, housing the J. A.
Freitas Library, at the corner of East 14th Street and Chu-
malia, in downtown San Leandro. (The building was dedicated
on March 13, 1971.) The second president of the association,
José Pimentel (1893-1894), San Leandro's first municipal
judge, designed the U. P. E. C. emblem and, upon the conclu-
sion of his term of office, became supreme secretary, a
post he held until his death on December 7, 1900. By this
time the society had spread throughout California. From a
single council in 1880 it had grown to 40 in 1899, with 3,004
members. On March 1, 1898, the first issue of the official
Boletim appeared in San Francisco under the editorship of
Mário Bettencourt de Câmara. Today, the Boletim, now
known as U. P. E. C. Life and published in both English and
Portuguese, has a circulation of about 6,000 copies and en-
joys the distinction of being the oldest magazine of its kind
in the United States. In 1902, King Carlos I of Portugal was
elected honorary president of the association, and the Portuguese government in turn honored the U. P. E. C. in 1935 and
again in 1966. Also in 1902, Oakland Council No. 24 organized a military team of twenty-five members with brilliant

uniforms, the Uniformed Corps of the U.P.E.C., which
was brought under the umbrella of the central office in the
same year and appeared with great lustre at public events.
In 1905 the justly famous U.P.E.C. Band was organized under the baton of Mário Bettencourt da Câmara, who conducted it until his death in 1936. In 1966, when the expense of
maintaining it proved burdensome, the band severed its connection with the U.P.E.C. and was transformed into the
San Leandro Municipal Band. The society grew spectacu-
larly, and by 1918 reached a membership of 12,491, the
highest on record. (In 1972 there were almost 11,000 members.) In 1928, when the idea of a health center was abandoned, a charity fund was created to help old U.P.E.C.
members in need of medical care. The increasing Americanization of the Portuguese community led to an amendment
to the by-laws in 1937 which permitted the use of English
whenever necessary. In 1946, English and Portuguese were
both declared the official languages. Originally, the U.P.
E.C. was limited to male adults only. Today, its membership is open to men as well as women and children, to Portuguese as well as non-Portuguese, but its Portuguese character remains unblemished. In 1974 its resources amounted
to $4,287,912.61 and it qualified as a non-profit, tax-exempt
insurance society.

1881   King Kalakaua of Hawaii traveled around the world, accompanied by William N. Armstrong, commissioner of immigration. The Hawaiian monarch was royally received in
Portugal. King Dom Luís I gave him a beautiful carriage
and silver harness, now on display in the Honolulu Museum.

January 27. José Gonçalves Correia was born in Flamengos,
Faial, Azores. He reached New Bedford, Massachusetts,
on board the Morning Star on August 13, 1901. He first
worked in local factories, then became a cooper. On May
13, 1908 he took to sea as a cooper on the brig Daisy, commanded by Captain Cleveland, the famous whaleman, and
went with him on trips to the Antarctic regions. In 1911 the
Daisy sailed for South Georgia with Correia on board and
also Robert Cushman Murphy, later to be connected with the
Museum of Natural History, New York. Correia became
Murphy's collaborator. (See Murphy's book, Logbook for
Grace [New York, 1947].) Mrs. Murphy, nee Grace E.
Barstow, in There's Always Adventure (New York, 1943),
refers to Correia as the man who prepared the most beauti-
ful animal skins in the world. On commission from the Mu-

seum of Natural History, Correia was in South Georgia
from November 22, 1913 to March 5, 1915, collecting birds
for the Museum. In 1919 he returned to the Azores for a
visit. In 1921, he went on an expedition for the Museum to
the eastern islands of the Atlantic to collect specimens of
their birds. He worked in Faial and Pico, Azores, then
moved to Madeira and the Canaries, and finally reach the
Cape Verdes. Upon his return from the trip, he was sent
to the islands of the Pacific on an expedition that lasted from
1923 to 1927. A new subspecies discovered by him in the
New Hebrides was named after him, G.f.correias. In 1926
he went on still another naturalist's hunt, to the South Pacific. He was back in the Azores for a family visit in 1927.
From the Azores, again commissioned by the Museum, he
sailed for São Tomé, Príncipe, Anobón, and Fernando Pó,
all in the Gulf of Guinea, in 1928, with a brief visit to Spanish Equatorial Guinea. He returned to the United States in
1930. In 1936 the Museum sent him on an expedition to Ariz-
ona. His last scientific expedition was in 1941, to Panamá
and Ecuador.

c. 1881   The short-lived O Luso-Americano, a Portuguese weekly
             newspaper, was founded in New Bedford, Massachusetts.

1882   Founding of the Monte Pio Luso-Americano, the oldest fra-
             ternal organization of New Bedford, Massachusetts. The
             society practices works of mercy under the patronage of St.
             Anthony of Padua, or of Lisbon, as he is known among the
             Portuguese. President McKinley authorized the Monte Pio
             to fly the Portuguese flag by itself, without the requirement
             of flying the American flag at the same time. Manuel M.
             Enos, the first president of the society, was given a knight-
             hood in the Order of Christ by King Dom Carlos I of Portu-
             gal in 1896.

             António F. Rodrigues, known as Antone F. Rogers, born in
             1866 on Flores, Azores, came to New Bedford, Massachu-
             setts about 1882 and to Little Compton, Rhode Island, in
             1891. In 1895 he bought the C.R. Wilbor farm on Maple
             Avenue. His son, Michael F. Rogers, owned the Little
             Compton Construction Company and the Fo'c's'le Restaurant.
             Michael's son, Richard, now runs the family's business in-
             terests.

             A. de Souza Canavarro was received by King Kalakaua on
             September 6 as the consul and commissioner of Portugal to
             the Kingdom of Hawaii.

1883   John B. Ávila, the "father of the sweet potato industry, " de-
              veloped the growing of sweet potatoes as a major commer-
              cial crop in the Atwater-Buhach area of California. Born on
              São Jorge, Azores, March 19, 1865, he got to California in
              1883, and died on November 25, 1937. He worked for five
              years on farms in southern Alameda County. In 1888, he
              and his brother bought twenty acres of irrigated land near
              Merced at $1.00 an acre where he planted sweet potatoes
              from the Azores and thus began the sweet potato industry
              of California. He was the first Portuguese to buy land in
              the Atwater-Buhach area. In 1902 Ávila entered into part-
              nership with three other Portuguese sweet potato growers,
              Frank Dutra, J. R. Trindade, and Frank M. Souza, the so-
              called "Big Four" who controlled the marketing of Atwater
              sweet potatoes for many years. From 1901 to 1921, when
              he retired, Ávila, together with J. J. Pimentel, ran a gen-
              eral merchandise store in Merced. He was one of the foun-
              ders of the Atwater branch of the Bank of America. In 1912-
              1913, he served as supreme president of the Irmandade do
              Divino Espírito Santo, an important California Portuguese
              association.

c. 1883   A Civilização Luso-Americana, a Portuguese newspaper,
              was published in Boston.

1884   May 16. Henry Freitas, the son of Portuguese immigrant
              parents, was born in Honolulu. From waterboy to one of
              the foremost contractors of Honolulu sums up the life of the
              late business executive, a graduate of St. Louis College.
              He is responsible for the following major building projects:
              Advertiser Publishing Company, Greater St. Louis College,
              E. O. Hal and Son Building, Piers 13 and 14, the Waialua
              branch of the Bishop National Bank, and the addition to Sa-
              cred Hearts Academy, Kaimuki. He also remodeled the
              Catholic Mission, Fort Street, Honolulu. Freitas served
              as a senator in the Territorial Legislature from 1953-1955.

              The Hawaii Homestead Law was passed. During 1886-1888,
              twenty Portuguese acquired lands under it in Oahu and Ha-
              waii.

              A Voz Portuguesa, the first Portuguese-language newspaper
              published in California, appeared in San Francisco under
              the editorship of António Maria Vicente, also known as Vi-
              cente da Virgem Maria, a native of Flores, Azores. (Other
              sources give Manuel Stone, a Brazilian, as the editor and

1880 as the date of its founding. In any event, its life was ephemeral.)

1884-1888   During these years, 925 Portuguese men, 638 Portuguese women, and 1,189 Portuguese children landed in Hawaii, at a cost of $144,249.99 to the government and $101,947.79 to the planters. The Portuguese were the chief source of labor in the islands, and the highest paid. In 1886, the government, for reason of economy, decided "that no further Portuguese immigrants were desired on the former terms. . . ."

c. 1884   Manuel Madruga, born in Ribeiras, Pico, Azores, in 1836, began the Portuguese settlement on Point Loma (San Diego). To escape military service at home, he served as a whaleman on an English ship, then deserted it in New Bedford, Massachusetts. Moving to Gloucester, Massachusetts, he became involved in the codfishing industry. A son, Manuel, Jr., later to become known as a designer and builder of ships in San Diego, was born in 1881. Rosalina, Madruga's wife, urged her husband to abandon fishing, and the family left for California. He worked in San Francisco for a Portuguese commission merchant and at his employer's suggestion, went to San Diego to begin a fishing business. Madruga settled in La Playa, on Point Loma. Here he salted and dried the fish that he caught and shipped it to San Francisco to his former boss. Within a few years other Portuguese arrived, all from Madruga's home parish. The family moved to nearby San Diego in 1909 or 1910 where they opened a general store at the corner of F and 6th streets. Later, Madruga started two fish markets, one for the wholesale trade (National Fish Company), the other a retail outlet. Madruga died in 1941 at the age of 105; his widow, in 1951, at the age of 101. Manuel, Jr., was in his nineties when Eduardo Mayone Dias interviewed him. Manuel Madruga is given credit as the founder of La Playa, a fashionable part of San Diego which has been described as the "ghetto" of the rich Portuguese families of the city. "A Portuguese by the name of Manuel Madruga, " Winifred Davison says in Where California Began (San Diego, 1929), "founded La Playa (the modern suburb of San Diego) as we know it . . . ." When the Madrugas moved to town, there were about 12 Portuguese families on Point Loma. The fifth generation of some of these families still lives in San Diego, where the Portuguese community, since enlarged by the arrival of new immigrants, now numbers about 8,000 people. It has become a remarkably prosperous ethnic ag-

glomeration, a number of whose members have amassed
sizable fortunes.

1885   There were a total of 21,293 Roman Catholics in Hawaii.
Of this number, 10,000 were Portuguese.

O Luso-Hawaiiano, a Portuguese-language newspaper, was
founded by A. Marques in Honolulu. It suspended publication in 1891. The last of the Portuguese newspapers of Hawaii came to an end in 1927.

José Tavares de Teves wrote "Um caso succedido" (An event
that happened), a series of narrative quatrains meant to be
sung in the Azorean manner, on Honokaa Plantation, October
15, 1885. It appeared in O Luso-Hawaiiano on November
5. The thirty-year-old poet had arrived from São Miguel,
Azores, on August 25, 1881.

António Maria Vicente and Manuel F.M. Trigueiro founded
the Portuguese-language newspaper, Progresso Californi-
ense, in San Francisco. It soon disappeared.

The Portuguese Roman Catholic parish of Our Lady of the
Rosary was founded in Providence, Rhode Island.

Out of 9,016 pupils in the Hawaiian schools, 1,185 were of
Portuguese nationality. Some of the largest schools of the
kingdom were made up almost entirely of Portuguese children.

1886-1888   The amount of $16,139.30 was spent on Portuguese immi-
gration in the Hawaiian Islands.

Three thousand, one hundred and thirty-two Portuguese
were employed on the plantations of the Hawaiian Islands.
The Chinese and Japanese, in that order, were numerically
more important.

1887   António Maria Vicente founded União Portuguesa, a Portuguese newspaper, in San Francisco. It was purchased by
Manuel F.M. Trigueiro in 1889 who continued to publish
until his death in 1940. The fiftieth anniversary of the newspaper was celebrated in 1938 with a commemorative issue
and a membership in the American Press Half Century Club.

July 11. Colton was incorporated as a city under the laws

of the state of California. The first known Portuguese settler, Manuel Goulart Soares, arrived in the same year.
His son-in-law, John Machado Coelho, a native of Raminho,
Terceira, Azores, was at one time president of the Colton
Rotary Club. In 1910, A.P. Gil, popularly known as Gill,
a native of Graciosa, Azores, operated the Anderson Barber Shop. In time he became the owner of the First National
Bank building. The Portuguese surnamed Dan Cunha built
the Colton Masonic Hall, completed in 1905, and designed
the old Colton City Hall.

The Portuguese Festival of the Divine Holy Ghost (Festa do
Divino Espírito Santo) is very much a part of the California
scene wherever the Portuguese have settled but nobody knows
exactly when and where the first such festival was held.
The first recorded one was in Sausalito, on San Francisco
bay, some time before 1887.

c. 1887   A group of Portuguese farmers in Mission San Jose, California, celebrated the Festival of the Divine Holy Ghost and
their action led ultimately to the founding of the Irmandade
do Divino Espírito Santo (Brotherhood of the Divine Holy
Ghost), an important Portuguese organization which continues to exist and is generally known by its initials I.D.E.S.
A first step was taken on July 7, 1889, when the Rev. Manuel Francisco Fernandes, then stationed at Mission San Jose,
called a meeting to discuss the saying of masses for the
souls of the departed members of a loosely knit brotherhood
that had earlier been founded, and the establishment of a
fund to aid the widows and children of deceased members.
The beginnings of the I.D.E.S. are clouded in mystery because the records are not complete, but the statutes (or
constitution) date from 1889. In June, 1891, the society
was formally incorporated under the title of Irmandade do
Divino Espírito Santo de Mission San Jose (Brotherhood of
the Divine Holy Ghost of Mission San Jose), Council No. 1.
Later it became known simply as the Irmandade do Divino
Espírito Santo (I.D.E.S.). The Supreme Council, created
in 1892, was moved from Mission San Jose to Centerville,
then to Hayward, and finally to Oakland, where it still is,
at 1110 Franklin Street. The first supreme president was
Manuel Silveira Peixoto, a native of Faial, Azores, who
served from the establishment of the Supreme Council to
1898. Until his death on January 22, 1922, he was the brotherhood's elder statesman. Council No. 2 was created
near Alvarado, October 31, 1892. The first annual conven-

tion was held at Mission San Jose, September 4, 1893. The third council was erected at Freeport, September 10, 1893; the fourth at Newark, the 5th at San Lorenzo, the 6th at Livermore, and the 7th at Antioch. A new I.D.E.S. constitution was published in 1896. In 1898, the traditional Festival of the Holy Ghost was cancelled because of the Spanish-American War and the drought in California. The society began to publish its Boletim (Bulletin) in 1899. From 1912 to his death in 1948, João C. Valim directed the society as supreme secretary. He is the author of the pioneer work on the history of the bortherhood, I.D.E.S. Apontamentos para a sua história (Oakland, 1922). The society reached its peak in 1917, with 11,006 members. In 1922, there were 1,295 non-Portuguese members. In 1964, the brotherhood had over 9,000 members and resources of over three million dollars. In 1965 it published the book that it had asked August Mark Vaz to write, The Portuguese in California, an enormously useful and revealing book that is indicative of the concern of the modern Portuguese-American for his American past.

1888   The first Portuguese Catholic church in California, the Church of the Holy Ghost, was inaugurated in Centerville. The first pastor was the Rev. Domingos Governo, a Portuguese. The church was later rebuilt by another Portuguese priest, the Rev. Alfredo M. de Sousa.

The discontinuance in this year of Portuguese sponsored immigration to Hawaii was the result of its high cost and the successful beginning of immigration from Japan.

1889   Manoel José de Freitas founded the Portuguese newspaper, Aurora Hawaiiana, in Honolulu. It came to an end in 1891.

1890   O Novo Mundo, a Portuguese-language newspaper, was founded in New Bedford, Massachusetts.

The oldest marching band in New England, the Santo Cristo Bank, which practices in the basement of Santo Cristo Church, Fall River, Massachusetts, celebrated its 85th anniversary in 1973. The band took an active part in the centennial celebrations of Fall River, 1911. In 1939 the famous band performed at the Portuguese Pavilion, New York World's Fair.

The Rev. João M. Tavares, a native of São Miguel, Azores,

one of the pioneer Catholic priests of California, began to
minister to the spiritual needs of the Portuguese of Oakland
at St. Mary's Church (Immaculate Conception), on Jefferson Street, between 7th and 8th streets. Later the Portuguese congregation met in the auditorium of St. Mary's Parochial School, at the corner of 7th and Grove streets. He
began to collect money for a Portuguese church and bought
a parcel of land near St. Mary's. Subsequently this land
was exchanged for the property on which the Portuguese
Church of St. Joseph was actually built. The dedicated Father Tavares died on February 1, 1891.

E.H. Cristiano was born in Santo António, Pico, Azores.
He emigrated to the United States in 1903 as a lad of 13.
After obtaining a degree in mining engineering and serving
in the United States Army during World War I, he studied
law. In 1920 he was admitted to the California Bar and in
the same year elected to the State Assembly. He was reelected in 1922. In 1924 he became a member of the California Senate.

1890-1900   With the partitioning and sale of the vast landed holdings of
J.W. Mitchell, many Portuguese during this decade moved
into the Atwater-Buhach area of Merced County, California.
Most of the pioneers were second generation California Portuguese.

1891   June 13. The first number of A Pátria, the first Portuguese
newspaper to be published in Oakland, California, appeared
on this day. It was founded by Manuel Stone, a Brazilian
national, and by the Sociedade de Publicidade Portuguesa.
It lasted for six years, coming to an end when Stone took
off for South Africa. By this time Oakland had become the
capital of the Portuguese in California. Over 4,000 of their
number lived there, mostly in West Oakland.

Guilherme M. Luiz, a native of Angra do Heroísmo, Azores,
arrived in the United States at the age of fourteen. He followed his fellow-Portuguese into the mills of New Bedford,
Massachusetts, where he settled. In 1909 the Luiz family
established the well-known Guilherme M. Luiz Travel
Agency of New Bedford and in 1919 founded A Alvorada,
which became the Diário de Notícias in 1920, the most ambitious and most professional newspaper ever published by
the Portuguese community of the United States.

February 21. The Rev. Manuel Francisco Fernandes, a pioneer Catholic priest of California, became pastor of the newly-organized Portuguese church of St. Joseph, Oakland. Born in Ribeiras, Pico, Azores in 1850, he emigrated to Brazil at the age of fourteen to seek his fortune. After six years, he returned to Pico, stayed three years, and then left for California. In Siskiyou he herded sheep and became the part-owner of a mine. Feeling the call of religion, he decided to prepare himself for the priesthood and went back to the Azores. Before doing so, he gave the land for the Church of the Immaculate Conception in Hawkinsville, Siskiyou County, which he helped to build. He was ordained to the priesthood by Archbishop William Patrick Riordan of San Francisco. His first assignment was Mission San Jose, where he stayed three years and founded the newspaper O Amigo dos Católicos. He was then transferred to Mendocino City. Later he spent a year observing missionary work in Honolulu and China. When he returned to California, he became Father Domingos Governo's assistant at the Centerville church. Upon the death of Father João Manual Tavares on February 1, 1891, he was sent to Oakland to head the new Portuguese parish. In the same year he built the Portuguese church of St. Joseph at a cost of $27,000 on Chestnut Street between 7th and 8th streets. He celebrated midnight mass in the new church on December 25,1891, in advance of its consecration by Archbishop Riordan on February 21, 1892. The rectory was built in 1893. He died on June 25, 1896. At his funeral mass, the Rev. Guilherme S. Glória, who was appointed to succeed him, gave homily and Archbishop Riordan presided. Before the Salesians took over the parish on September 11, 1902, five Portuguese diocesan priests served as pastors. The church no longer exists, but in the course of its history many important events were centered there. In 1907 Bishop Henrique Silva celebrated mass on several occasions. In 1910 the church honored the officers and crew of the São Gabriel, a Portuguese cruiser on a courtesy visit to San Francisco. The silver anniversary of the church was celebrated in 1917, with the presence of Archbishop Edward Hanna of San Francisco. In 1932, the church commemorated the death of St. Anthony of Lisbon (or St. Anthony of Padua, the most universally beloved of all Portuguese saints, who died in Italy in 1231), a festival that was repeated in 1935. In 1936, the sixth centenary of the death of Queen St. Elizabeth of Portugal (after whom the oldest of the Portuguese women's beneficent socieites of California is named), was brilliantly celebrated. Dom Manuel Gonçalves Cerejeira, the Cardinal Patriarch of Lisbon, came to Oakland for the festivities at the invitation of the Sociedade Portuguesa Rainha Santa Isabel. The pastoral statistics for the Portuguese Church of St. Joseph, 1891-1942, follow: marriages celebrated, 6,520; baptisms, 13,266; funerals, 6,498; first holy communions, 3,760; confirmations, 2,379; and sick calls, 4,915.

1892   J. M. Vivas began the publication in Honolulu of A Sentinella, which ceased publication in 1896.

The 350th anniversary of the discovery of California by the Portuguese navigator, João Rodrigues Cabrilho, was festively celebrated in San Diego, September 28-30. Governor Markham was in attendance. Plans for the 400th anniversary, scheduled for 1942, were cancelled because of the Second World War.

The last of the California whaling stations, at San Simeon, closed. It was founded in 1865 by an Azorean Portuguese, José Machado, known as Joseph Clark.

The first Ph. D. dissertation on a Portuguese subject in the United States was by Edward Gaylord Bourne of Yale University, "The Demarcation Line of Pope Alexander VI." Between 1892-1970, 263 dissertations on Portuguese or Portuguese-related topics were written in the United States, Canada, and Great Britain. There have been 419 on the history of Brazil since the arrival in Rio de Janeiro of the Portuguese royal family in 1808. Among the Portuguese-surnamed authors, 22 wrote on Portuguese topics, 32 on Brazilian topics (since 1808). Of the universities listed in the survey, Columbia leads the list with 62, Wisconsin is second with 38, California third with 33, Harvard fourth with 27, Florida fifth with 24, Pennsylvania sixth with 19.

c. 1892   The first Portuguese who came to San Diego were whalemen: Manuel M. Medina, José M. Medina, João M. Medina, and Francisco Theodoro, all of Ballast Point. Later, M. Silveira Soares, João Moniz, António Moniz, José V. Soares, José Monteiro, and Frank Goulart arrived on the scene and settled in La Playa.

1893   A whaleman from Faial, Azores, with a corrupted Portuguese name, Joseph Silvia, settled in New London, Connecticut about 1863. In 1893 he moved to Little Compton,

Rhode Island, where his son, Frank A. Silvia, was the
first Portuguese elected to the town council (1937-1940).
Another Portuguese, Manuel Cotta, a native of Doze Ribeiras, Terceira, Azores, served on the same council from
1940 to 1948.

The Portuguese church of Freeport, California, was consecrated in September. The Rev. Guilherme S. Glória said
the mass.

1894   A Provincetown, Massachusetts, newspaper had this to say
            about its fishing fleet, "In model, rig and fishing methods,
            our [Grand Banks fishing | fleet conforms to the fleets of
            other fishing ports, but in the matter of crews it is strik-
            ingly different. Other fleets are sailed by men of all na-
            tions, no one race predominating largely, but the Province-
            town fleet is manned exclusively by Portuguese . . . . Cap-
            tains and crews are all, or nearly all, Azoreans, and from
            a mere handful in 1840, the Portuguese population has in-
            creased to upward of 2,000 in 1894. Not all of these are na-
            tives of the Western Islands, a large portion were born here.
            But born in America or the Azores, they take kindly to the
            sea, and make excellent fishermen."

            Manuel Alves Faria, a native of Bretanha, São Miguel,
            Azores, arrived in the United States at the age of fourteen.
            Four years later he married Ermelinda Raposo, also of
            São Miguel, and in 1904 returned to the Azores. They were
            back in Fall River, Massachusetts in 1915. A son, José
            Faria, graduated from the B.M.C. Durfee High School, Fall
            River, in 1929, attended Bryant College evening classes,
            and from 1936-1945 became a public accountant in Fall Ri-
            ver. For eleven years he was a wholesale liquor dealer.
            In time he became director of the Fall River Trust Com-
            pany; in 1966, vice chairman of the board; and in 1968,
            chairman and chief executive officer.

1895   A Chronica, a humorous and satirical journal, edited by
            Mário Bettencourt da Câmara, was founded in San Francis-
            co. After fourteen numbers, A Chronica, the first news-
            paper of its kind in California, became a victim of the bit-
            terness of its attacks on the local Portugues colony and died.

            The Kalihi Holy Ghost Society was founded in Honolulu to
            celebrate feasts of the liturgical calendar and sponsor so-
            cial activities.

A local and independent organization, the Sociedade do Espírito Santo (S.E.S.) was founded in Santa Clara, California. Despite early difficulties, the society still exists.

1895-1911   Five hundred and fourteen Portuguese took up 18,096 acres of homestead lands in the Hawaiian Islands.

1896   A União Lusitano-Hawaiiana and A Sentinella, both of Honolulu, merged to form O Luso. First edited by J.S. Ramos, the Portuguese newspaper continued until 1924.

O Direito was founded in Honolulu by A.J. Rego and was published until 1898. In the same year, and also in Honolulu, A.H.R. Vieira started still another Portuguese newspaper, As Boas Novas, which lasted until 1905.

June 26. The death occurred of the Rev. Manuel Francisco Fernandes, pastor of the Portuguese church of St. Joseph, Oakland, California. He was succeeded by another Portuguese priest, also a native of the Azores, the Rev. Guilherme S. Glória, who resigned in 1899 to return to private life. On May 20, 1898, the church liturgically celebrated the fourth centennial of Vasco da Gama's voyage to India with ceremonies presided over by Archbishop William Patrick Riordan of San Francisco. The music for the solemn mass was directed by Mário Bettencourt da Câmara.

1897   August 10. The first issue appeared of O Reporter, founded in California by Mr. and Mrs. Constantino C. Soares and Attorney Frank Joseph. The Portuguese-language newspaper was sold in 1910 to the Rev. José Silva. In 1914 António Conceição Teixeira bought a half interest in it and managed it for about three months. It came to an end in 1916.

1898   March 15. A group of thirty pious women under the leadership of Rosa M. Oliveira met on this day to form an altar society to serve the Portuguese Church of St. Joseph, Oakland, California, and at the same time to provide sick and death benefits to the members. This was the beginning of the Sociedade Portuguesa Rainha Santa Isabel (Portuguese Society of Queen St. Elizabeth), generally known by the initials S.P.R.S.I., the most prestigious Portuguese women's organization in the United States named after the holy queen of medieval Portugal who was canonized in 1625. The original group, which terminated its connection with the church

three years later, became Council No. 1 of the association.
By 1900, six other councils had been started. In April, 1900,
the statutes of the S.P.R.S.I. were revised and the decision
was made to recruit members throughout California. On
January 20, 1901, the Supreme Council was organized. So
rapid was the growth of the society that forty-seven new
councils were formed in 1901. In the same year, the official Boletim (Bulletin) of the S.P.R.S.I. began to be published. In 1928 a charity fund was established, to aid needy
members. In 1936 the society celebrated the sixth centenary of the death of its patron with a grand religious celebration in Oakland, presided over by Dom Manuel Gonçalves
Cerejeira, the Cardinal Patriarch of Lisbon. In line with
its strong cultural concerns, the society has awarded scholarships to high school graduates, children of its members,
since 1950. For many years the affairs of the society were
directed by Mrs. Leopoldina C. Rodrigues Alves, a native
of the Azores, in her capacity as supreme secretary. The
central offices are at 3031 Telegraph Avenue, Oakland.
The 74th annual convention of the organization was held in
1974. At that time there were 13,503 members and resources totalling $5,315.323. No Portuguese society in the
United States has so large a membership or is more prosperous.

March 1. The first number of the offical Boletim (Bulletin)
of the União Portuguesa do Estado da California, edited by
Mário Bettencourt da Câmara, appeared in San Francisco.
The initial circulation was 2,500 copies at a cost of $18.30
per press run. The magazine, now known as U.P.E.C.
Life, has a present-day circulation of 6,000 copies and en-
joys the distinction of being the oldest publication of a Portuguese fraternal, civic, and social nature in the United
States. Today, the magazine serves not only as a house
organ, with U.P.E.C. information for the benefit of the
members, but also as a vehicle for articles on the history
of the Portuguese presence in California. As an historical
journal, its position is also unrivalled.

The Rev. A. Domingos de Campos, a native of Portugal, became the third pastor of the Portuguese church of St. Joseph,
Oakland, California, in this year. Because of ill health, he
retired to Sacramento after only one year and five months
in office, where he died. The fourth pastor of the church
was another Portuguese priest, the Rev. Dario Raposo, who
served from December 28, 1900 to September 11, 1902,

when the parish was turned over to the Salesian Fathers. The next pastor was an Italian, Father Felice Andrea Bergeretti, a former apostolic missionary in Ceylon, India, Australia, and Palestine. With his death in 1909, another Italian Salesian, Father José Galli, who had spent some time in Portugal and spoke Portuguese, became pastor. As Father Bergeretti's assistant and later as pastor in his own right, Father Galli served the church for thirty years, until 1947, when he asked to be relieved of his duties for reasons of health.

September 29. Manuel C. Rosa, a patent law attorney with the Department of Commerce, Washington, D.C., was born in Taunton, Massachusetts. Rosa has been a member of the examining corps in the Patent Office for more than thirty-five years. He is best known for a classification of organic compounds (1938) which is still used today. In 1951 he became director of Patent Examining, Classifying and Research Activities in the Patent Office. He received a medal for meritorious service from the Department of Commerce in 1953 and a gold medal for exceptional service in 1957. He has written extensively on patent law and had lectured widely on the subject.

October 3. Isabel Soares, the wife of M.O. Medina, the pioneer Portuguese founder of the tuna industry in San Diego, was born, like her husband, in Santa Cruz das Ribeiras, Pico, Azores. (They were both born in the same house and room, their grandmothers having been twin-sisters.) Losing her mother at the time of her birth, young Isabel left the Azores for San Diego to be with her uncle and aunt, José and Perpétua Soares. She was educated in a one-room schoolhouse on Point Loma. She joined the California Portuguese women's organization, the União Portuguesa Protectora do Estado da Califórnia (U.P.P.E.C.) and served, first, as its supreme president, 1939-1940, and in the following year as a supreme director. Always interested in Portuguese activities and concerned about the spread of Portuguese culture in America, she increased her effectiveness through foreign travel, to Europe and South America, in 1936, 1949, 1955, and 1967. Mrs. Medina continues to be one of the first ladies of the California Portuguese community and of San Diego.

António H. Rosa, a native of New Bedford, Massachusetts, Fall River's first Portuguese physician, graduated in this year from the School of Medicine, University of Maryland, Baltimore.

1899-1927   Three Portuguese newspapers were published in Hilo, Hawaii: A Voz Pública (1899-1904), A Setta (1903-1921), and O Facho (1906-1927). With the demise of O Facho, the Portuguese press of Hawaii came to an end.

1900   The first class in Portuguese in the state of California was started in Sacramento.

Only one out of sixty-two medical doctors in Fall River, Massachusetts, were of Portuguese descent. Among the school teachers, there were only seven. In 1973, nearly 20 percent of the teachers are of Portuguese ancestry.

October 1. The first issue of A Liberdade, a Portuguese weekly edited by Guilherme Silveira da Glória, appeared in Sacramento, California. Glória moved the editorial offices to Oakland in 1920 and for the next six years the newspaper was published daily (except Sundays). Thereafter it returned to the weekly format. Glória, a former Catholic priest, suspended publication at the end of 1936, following the death of his wife and son. Born in Candelária, Pico, Azores, on July 6, 1863, he began his theological training at the Angra Episcopal Seminary, Terceira, Azores, and finished it at St. Thomas Seminary, Mission San Jose, California. He was ordained by Archbishop William Patrick Riordan of San Francisco on June 29, 1885, being assigned as a curate to the only parish that then existed in San Leandro. In 1895 he became the pastor of the parish of San Pablo and in 1896 of the Portuguese Church of St. Joseph, Oakland. Secularized in 1899, he married shortly thereafter. He regularized his canonical situation in 1939, when, at his request, he was reduced to the lay state. He published two volumes of poetry in the Portuguese language. Poemas (Oakland, 1935) contains miscellaneous rimes and a six-canto epic, in the style of Luís de Camões, on João Rodrigues Cabrilho, the Portuguese discoverer of California. Harpejos was published in Oakland in 1940. The biography of Glória is by the Rev. José Carlos, of the Portuguese church of Turlock, California, Padres da Ilha do Pico alunos no Seminário Episcopal de Angra subsídios biográficos, I (n.p., 1970), pp. 114-118.

The Hawaiian Portuguese newspaper, A Liberdade, edited

by C. Pereira, was published in Honolulu during the years 1900-1910.

1900-1925   During these years between 1,000 and 1,500 Cape Verdeans entered the United States as immigrants. In 1930, only 63.

1900-1930   Until 1900, 85 percent of the Portuguese settlers of the San Joaquin valley, California, were from the Azorean islands of Pico, Faial, São Jorge, Flores, and Corvo. From 1910-1930, the pattern changed. Sixty percent of the Portuguese settling in the central valley were from the Azorean island of Terceira.

1901   Frank M. Silvia, of Fall River, Massachusetts, died. He was a leading representative of the Portuguese community of Bristol county. He was born on São Jorge, Azores, March 2, 1850, took to the sea at the age of twelve, circumnavigated the globe, and first settled in New Bedford. The Silvias were one of the first four Portuguese families in Fall River. The youngest son of the Silvia family, John A. Silvia, was the first person of Portuguese descent from Fall River to be ordained a Roman Catholic priest.

José Peixoto Pinheiro, a Portuguese pioneer of Hanford, California, was born in São Roque, Pico, Azores, on September 20, 1861. He married Maria Paulina Pinheiro in 1900 and left for California in the following year. He went back to the Azores in 1906 and in 1907 returned to California with his wife and daughter, settling in Hanford. He opened up a grocery store in 1913. From 1915-1916 he served as supreme president of the Irmandade do Divino Espírito Santo (I.D.E.S.) and later as supreme secretary of the Portuguese benevolent association.

February 4. Sixty-four Portuguese women, under the leadership of Mrs. Maria C. Leal Soares Fenn, met in Oakland to found an association dedicated to social and charitable works under the patronage of Our Lady of the Immaculate Conception. Thus began the Portuguese women's benevolent society, União Portuguesa Protectora do Estado da Califórnia (U.P.P.E.C.), with headquarters today at 12229 B Street, Hayward, California. By July 21, fifteen councils were in existence, and on August 12, delegates of these councils met in Oakland to create the Supreme Council and to elect Mrs. Fenn as the first supreme president. The society was incorporated under the laws of the state of California on January 25, 1902. In the same year, Queen Dona Amélia of Portugal accepted the honorary supreme presidency of the U.P.P.E.C. The official bulletin of the society dates from 1912. In 1957, the first youth council was started, in Hayward. Eleven such councils were functioning in 1974. In 1965 a scholarship program was launched, designed to help worthy high school graduates, members of the society, pursue their education. In 1974, the U.P.P.E.C. also had ninety-four regular councils throughout California, with more than 9,000 members. Reserve assets of the society, as of May 31, 1974, amounted to $3,071,721.79. Although the society continues to be run for and by women -- Mrs. Lena B. Fraga is the supreme secretary -- men and boys have been eligible for insurance protection since 1969.

1902   April 12. Judge Cyrus Nils Tavares, son of Antone Ferreira Tavares, was born at Pukalani, Maui, Hawaii. A 1925 law graduate of the University of Michigan, he received an honorary doctorate of law from his alma mater in 1963. He was admitted to the Hawaiian Bar in 1925. From 1927-1934, he was deputy attorney general of Hawaii; 1942-1943, assistant attorney general; and 1944-1947, attorney general. From 1960 until his retirement in 1972, he was United States district judge, Hawaii. In 1950 he was a delegate to the Hawaiian Constitutional Convention. He has served as special counsel to the House of Representatives and Senate of Hawaii. In 1953-1956 he was chairman of the Hawaii Statehood Commission. He is a past president of the Bar Association of Hawaii. Judge Tavares is listed in Who's Who in America. No Hawaiian of Portuguese ancestry has had a more brilliant legal career.

The first edition of a Portuguese Protestant hymnal was printed by the Typographia Lusitana, Honolulu, for the Hawaiian Missionary Board, Canticos Evangelicos, Nova Collecção de Psalmos e Hymnos. A second edition, printed by the Mercantile Printing Company, Ltd., Honolulu, was published in 1916. One of the translators of the lyrics and composers of some of the songs was A.H.R. Vieira (1874-1934).

1903   O Imparcial, a Portuguese newspaper, was founded by Manuel S. Quaresma, a pioneer Portuguese printer, in Sacramento, California. He sold it in 1930 and the new owners continued to publish it until 1932.

From 1903-1919, 12,522 Cape Verdeans emigrated to the
United States. The Cape Verdeans were known by the generic name of Bravas, after the name of one of the islands
of the archipelago.

1904   The Rev. Roberto K. Baptista, a native of Jacksonville,
Illinois, and a descendant of Madeiran Protestants who set-
tled in Illinois before the Civil War, founded the Portuguese
Methodist Church in Oakland, California.

The fourth edition of a catechism for Portuguese Catholics,
Catecismo Pequeno da Doutrina Christã, was published by
A Liberdade Publishing Company, Ltd., Honolulu.

A facsimile edition of the Cancioneiro geral or songbook of
Garcia de Resende (Lisbon, 1516) was published at the expense of Archer M. Huntington, founder of the Hispanic Society of America, New York.

1905   January 1. The private hospital of St. Anthony, Oakland,
California, was founded by a group of prominent Portuguese
headed by Dr. M.M. Enos. This was the first Portuguese
hospital of California. In 1924 the hospital had 100 beds
and a special maternity ward.

January 18. The "A Pátria" Association of Mutual Help was
founded in Honolulu. It was incorporated on December 10,
1910. The original constitution and statutes are in Portuguese. One of the founders was José Coelho de Sousa (1880-
1950).

The Portuguese-American Bank of San Francisco was organized.

Pedro Laureano Claudino Silveira, a native of São Jorge,
Azores, one of the first Portuguese printers of California,
founded Portugal-América in Fresno, a Portuguese newspaper of ephemeral history.

May 24. Justice George Perry Ponte, a member of a distinguished Portuguese-American family, was born in New
Bedford, Massachusetts. His parents, Joseph Ponte and
Maria R. Freitas, were natives of the Azores. He earned
a law degree from Boston University in 1927 and in the same
year was admitted to the Massachusetts Bar. He was a
member of the city council, New Bedford from 1928 to 1930,

and from 1938 to 1942, president of the council, 1942.
From 1943 to 1944, he served in the Massachusetts House
of Representatives. He became an associate justice of the
Superior Court of the Commonwealth of Massachusetts in
1963. His present term on the high bench expires in 1975.

December 2. George Ernest Freitas, the son of Henry
Freitas, the well-known builder, was born in Honolulu.
He graduated in civil engineering from the University of
Dayton in 1929. He founded the Pacific Construction Com-
pany, 1938, and served as chairman and director until 1969.

1906   During 1906-1909, 3,403 Portuguese arrived in Hawaii.

1907   May 17. The great Azorean liturgical feast of Santo Cristo
            (Ecce Homo), a particular devotion of the people of São
            Miguel, was celebrated by the Salesian Fathers in the Por-
            tuguese Church of St. Joseph, Oakland, California. The mass
            was celebrated by Bishop Henrique J. Reed da Silva, titular
            bishop of Trajanopolis, from Portugal, who was on a visit
            to the United States. The sermon was preached by the Rev.
            Domingos Governo, of Centerville.

1908   The Portuguese-language weekly, As Novidades, began to
            be published in Fall River, Massachusetts, by John Machado.
            It came to an end in 1940.

            A Voz da Verdade, a Portuguese-language newspaper owned
            by M.C. Simas, began to be published in May in Oakland,
            California. It lasted a year.

            Archbishop William Patrick Riordan of San Francisco was
            asked by the 694 Portuguese of Buhach, Franklin, and Atwater,
            California, to authorize the establishment of a church for
            the Portuguese Catholics of the area. The church was star-
            ted in 1909 with the Rev. Alfred M. Souza as the first pas-
            tor. In 1910 he was succeeded by the Rev. Joseph Cunha,
            in turn succeeded by the Rev. Henry A. Ribeiro, the latter
            serving until 1914. On December 3,1922, with the creation
            of the diocese of Monterey-Fresno, the Atwater-Buhach par-
            ish became part of the new ecclesiastical division. In 1925
            the church at Atwater was moved to its present location.
            John B. Ávila, António J. Noya, and Frank Dutra were the
            early leaders of the Catholic and Portuguese population of
            Merced County.

Between 1908-1919, no Portuguese in Hawaii returned to the land of their birth.

1909

The first Festival of the Holy Ghost (Festa do Espírito Santo), a traditional religious celebration of the Portuguese Atlantic islands, was held in La Playa, on San Diego bay, and brought together the Portuguese people of La Playa, Roseville, and San Diego proper. It has been held on Point Loma ever since. The pioneer festa was organized by a pious fisherman from the Cape Verde Islands, Francisco Silva, whose daughter, Rose, was the first festival queen.

October 13. A parade and celebration in Oakland, California, commemorated the restoration of Portugal on December 1, 1640. Among those who took part in the parade were the chief of police, local officials, many marching bands, the Uniformed Corps of the U.P.E.C., and delegations from the several Portuguese fraternal societies.

October 15. The Rev. João Vieira de Azevedo founded the Portuguese Church of St. Elizabeth, Sacramento, California.

1910

The first Portuguese school in the United States, an adjunct of Santo Cristo parish, Fall River, Massachusetts, opened its doors. The man most responsible for it was the parish's second pastor, the Rev. João B. de Valles, a chaplain hero in the First World War whose name is perpetuated in a New Bedford, Massachusetts, public school.

Ezra Pound, the American poet, devoted a chapter to the Portuguese epic, Luís de Camões (1524?-1580), in his Spirit of Romance. Pound worked up the love story of Dom Pedro, the crown prince of Portugal, and Inês de Castro, a lady-in-waiting at court, as told by Camões in The Lusiads (1572), years later in Canto 30 (after alluding to it in Canto 12).

Dr. John C. Branner, the second president of Stanford University, with a background of geological exploration in Brazil, published A Brief Grammar of the Portuguese language with Exercises and Vocabularies (New York: Henry Holt and Company). His extensive Brasiliana, also rich in Portuguese items, was acquired by the Stanford University Library.

c. 1910

The Kewale Holy Ghost was founded in Honolulu to mark the feasts of the liturgical year, such as the traditional Portu-

guese celebration of Christmas and the seven domingas
within the octave of Easter.

1911   In this year two sons of Portuguese immigrants, Joseph
              Soares and Anthony de Mello, served as deputy sheriff and
              deputy auditor, respectively, of Alameda County, California.
              Manuel Riggs, also of Portuguese descent, was chief engineer
              of the Hayward Fire Department. After World War I, Louis
              Silva, of Portuguese-Mexican ancestry, became chief of po-
              lice of Hayward.

              Because of poor working conditions on the plantations of
              Hawaii, 2,000 Portuguese left the islands for California be-
              tween 1911-1914.

              O Popular, a Portuguese-language newspaper, was published
              in Honolulu by J.S. Ramos. It came to an end in 1913.

              The Companhia Editora do Pacifico, Honolulu, published the
              Almanach Portuguez de Hawaii para 1911 um Livro de re-
              ferencia e Informação Geral Relativo ao Territorio de Ha-
              waii, Portugal, Madeira, e Açores. The work was written
              by M.G. Santos (1871-1932).

              With the support of the União Portuguesa do Estado da Cali-
              fórnia (U.P.E.C.) and of the Irmandade do Divino Espírito
              Santo (I.D.E.S.), João C. Valim founded the António Fonte
              Portuguese School, named after the first supreme president
              of the U.P.E.C., in the rectory of St. Joseph's Church,
              Oakland, California. It was designed to teach the mother
              tongue to children between the ages of ten and twelve as
              well as the history and geography of Portugal and the Azores.
              The school was in existence for a little more than a year.

              From 1911 to 1930, the per capita assessed valuation on
              personal property owned by the Portuguese in Hawaii rose
              from $21.44 to $53.69; on real estate, from $105.80 to
              $522.62. The Portuguese were above the Chinese and
              Japanese in 1911, slightly under the Chinese in 1930.

1912   O Lavrador Português, a Portuguese newspaper, was founded
              in Lemoore, California, by Artur Vieira de Ávila, João de
              Melo, and Constantinto Barcelos. When it moved to Hanford,
              Ávila became the sole editor. In 1920 it was moved again,
              this time to Tulare, where Ávila and Alfredo Silva joined
              forces in putting it out. The two editors took it with them
              to Oakland in 1927.

1913   February 26. A group of Madeirans, meeting in West Oakland, California, founded the Associação Protectora União
Madeirense do Estado da Califórnia, a social and benevolent society known by the shortened title of União Madeirense. The official date of its founding is March 13, 1913,
but there is reason to believe that it began a fortnight earlier. The first supreme secretary was António da Conceição Teixeira, who became a member in 1914. In 1936
the União Madeirense purchased the building in Fruitvale,
Oakland, which continues as its headquarters. At the time
of the Golden Jubilee of 1963, the União Madeirense had
thirty-six councils, composed of men, women, and young
people, largely in California but also in Massachusetts,
Rhode Island, and Hawaii. The society is intended primarily for Portuguese of Madeiran birth or origin.

A native of Faial, Azores, João Francisco Escobar, was the
author of The new method to learn the Portuguese language
without teacher; with figurated pronunciation of tones and
sounds, published in New Bedford, Massachusetts.

1914   Joseph C. Carvalho, a native of São Miguel, Azores, and a
resident of Fall River, Massachusetts, graduated in dentis-
try from the University of Maryland. He was the first Fall
River male of Portuguese descent to become a dentist.

Cândido da Costa Nunes founded A Califórnia Alegre. The
periodical was sporadically published in Oakland and then
at Lemoore, Tulare, and Hanford before returning to Oakland, where it died.

A Portuguese monthly, A Revista Portuguesa, appeared in
Hayward, California. João de Melo managed to publish it
until 1925.

Mr. A. de Souza Canavarro, who had served for twenty-
eight years as the consul of Portugal in Hawaii, died.

O Portugal, a weekly Portuguese newspaper, was founded in
New Bedford, Massachusetts, by Alberto Moura, a native of
Chaves, Portugal, who had arrived in the United States in
the same year. In 1916 he sold the newspaper and moved
to California, where he was destined to spend the rest of
his days.

1915   A Portuguese weekly newspaper, O Mundo, was published in California by Joaquim Oliveira, who gave it up very shortly for reasons of health and went to New Bedford, Massachusetts, where he died.

Among the Portuguese of Massachusetts, there were 27 clergymen, 1 actor, 8 musicians, 8 physicians and surgeons, 9 teachers, 5 trained nurses, 10 dentists, 1 lawyer, 52 bartenders, 440 servants, 25 waiters, and 5 saloon keepers.

1916   In this year the Sociedade de Caridade Portuguesa (Portuguese Charity Society) came into existence in Honolulu.

By this year the Portuguese of California had reached a high level of prosperity. In Los Banos, an agricultural community of 4,000 inhabitants, many Portuguese owned dairies and occupied positions of responsibility. The Gomes brothers owned a dairy ranch valued at $100,000, and other Portuguese, such as A.J. Azevedo, were also people of means.

António Rogers, born Soares, a pioneer leader of San Leandro, California, died in April. Born in Flamengos, Faial, Azores, in 1835, he left his native land at the age of thirteen on board a Yankee whaler. In 1859 Rogers gave up the life of the sea and moved to California, settling in San Leandro on San Francisco bay. His son, António Agostinho Rogers, known as Antone Augustine Rogers and as A.A. Rogers, was born in San Leandro in 1875. He was admitted to the California Bar in 1908 and in the following year became deputy district attorney of Alameda County. He was elected to the State Assembly on the Republican ticket in November, 1910, and served a two-year term. He resigned his political offices in 1920 to devote himself to the practice of law.

André Azevedo, a native of São Jorge, Azores, was a merchant in Novato, California, secretary of the Irmandade do Divino Espírito Santo (I.D.E.S.), and a director of the Bank of Novato. The population of the place was largely Portuguese.

May 14. The Portuguese Hotel, a landmark on Clay Street, San Francisco, was the scene of a great banquet in honor of Carlos Rangel Sampaio, the consul of Portugal. Many of the important people of the Portuguese colony were in attendance. The menu was patriotically Portuguese, featuring dishes from the Azores, Madeira, and Portugal. All the wines were Portuguese and the coffee, at the end, was Brazilian.

Dr. Manoel de Oliveira Lima (1867-1928), the distinguished
Brazilian diplomat, historian, and journalist of Portuguese
antecedents -- his father was born in Portugal as was one
of his maternal grandparents -- offered his rich library to
The Catholic University of America, Washington, D.C. The
offer was accepted by the Board of Trustees, the books and
other objects were brought from Europe to America, and in
1924 the Oliveira Lima Library was formally opened to the
public. This oldest and most prestigious of the great Luso-
Brazilian libraries of the United States comprises over
50,000 printed books, thousands of manuscripts, and a large
iconographical and museum collection. A catalogue of the
library's holdings, in two volumes, was published by G.K.
Hall & Co., of Boston, in 1970.

1917   January 28. Twenty-seven continentals, i.e. natives of
continental Portugal, met at St. Joseph's Portuguese Church,
Oakland, California, to organize their own benevolent society
under the leadership of Joaquim dos Santos Oliveira, João
Roldão, and Manuel Gomes Soares. Thus began the União
Portuguesa Continental do Estado da Califórnia (Portuguese
Continental Union of the State of California), for many years
known simply as U.P.C. There were already other Portuguese socieities in existence but they were controlled by
the California Portuguese of Azorean or Madeiran origin.
The idea of a separate organization was first proposed by
José Rodrigues Drack in 1916. Because of the relatively
few continentals in California, the society decided to enlarge the geographical area of its activities by including
the East Coast. On April 24, 1919, Alberto Moura, a young
law student who had become the secretary of the U.P.C.,
was sent to New England, where he organized two councils,
one in Plymouth, Massachusetts, and one in Pawtucket, Rhode
Island. In time other councils of the California-based society were created in Massachusetts, Rhode Island, Connecticut, New York, and New Jersey. A supreme council, with
headquarters in Oakland, was organized in 1922. On November 1, 1925, a group of Portuguese immigrants from Massachusetts founded their own regional society, and on October
1, 1929 the União Portuguesa Continental dos Estados Unidos
da América (Portuguese Continetal Union of the United
States of America) was incorporated under the laws of the
Commonwealth of Massachusetts. A number of eastern
councils severed their connection with the California society and joined the new association, but other councils retained their affiliation. On July 1, 1957, the U.P.C. merged

with the Benevolent Society of California to form, on the national level, the United National Life Insurance Society and,
within California, the Luso-American Fraternal Federation.
The last surviving founding member of the U.P.C. and its
first president, Artur Nunes Alegrete, died in Lisbon, July
8, 1974.

May 13. On a mountain meadow in the Portuguese midlands,
three children, aged ten, nine, and seven, reported seeing
a lady while tending their flocks. The last apparition was
on October 13. In subsequent years the shrine and pilgri-
mage center of Our Lady of Fátima was built on the spot.
where Our Lady was said to have appeared, and thus began
the great Marian devotion of the twentieth century, a devotion which has affected the spiritual life of the Portuguese
communities in the United States. At least four Portuguese-
Americans have published works on Fátima. Monsignor
Joseph Cacella is the author of two books: Our Lady of Fatima (New York, 1946) and The Wonders of Fatima (New
Yor, 1948). Humberto S. Medeiros (now the Cardinal Archbishop of Boston) and William F. Hill wrote Jacinta, The
Flower of Fátima (New York, 1946), based on a Portuguese
work by Jose Galambra de Oliveira. Manoel Cardozo, of
the Catholic University of America, is the author of the pre-
faceto the late George C.A. Boehrer's translation of Idalino
da Costa Brochado's book which appeared in English under
the title of Fátima in the light of history (Milwaukee, 1955).
Asdrúbal Castello Branco was among the arrangers of John
de Marchi's The Crusade of Fatima. The Lady More Brilliant than the Sun (New York, 1948), orginally issued in
Portuguese.

When the United States entered the First World War, over
15,000 Portuguese volunteered for service in the armed
forces. The first American soldier to fall in the war was
Walter Goulart, a Portuguese-American. There is a monument to his memory in New Bedford, Massachusetts.

The Camões Chair of Portuguese Studies was established
at King's College, London. Until the appointment of Edgar
Prestage in 1923, the chair was held by William Bentley.
In 1938, with Professor Prestage's retirement, the chair
was offered to Manoel da Silveira Cardozo, then working
in Lisbon on his Stanford University doctor's degree in history, who turned it down for personal reasons.

In 1917, two Portuguese served in the Hawaiian Senate; in 1921-1927, one; in 1931-1932, one; and in 1953, two. In 1932, the sergeant-at-arms of the Senate was a Portuguese.

A Portuguese-language school, financed by the Portuguese government, was opened in Honolulu.

1918   February 24. Mrs. Maria Josefina da Glória founded the Luís da Camões Portuguese Library in Oakland, California. It was in operation as late as 1939.

1919   May 11. José Madeira Feliciano, a prominent contractor and businessman of the Washington metropolitan area, was born in Casal Pardo, Alfeizarão, district of Leiria, Portugal, the son of a road builder and farmer. Arriving in the United States in 1944, he became a seaman (later a chief cook) with the Maritime Commission. In 1952, the year before he became an American citizen, he founded the Lisbon Construction Company of Kensington, Maryland, now Lisbon Madeira, Ltd., of which he is president. The firm has built highways, streets, bridges, sewers, etc., in Maryland and the District of Columbia, including a Maryland section of Interstate 495 (Washington Beltway). At the present time the firm is working on a water filtration plant and sewer lines in Maryland.

July 13. The Igreja das Cinco Chagas, the Church of the Five Wounds, of San Jose, California, the grandest church ever built by the Portuguese in California, was consecrated by Monsignor Henrique Augusto Ribeiro. The present pastor, the Rev. Carlos B. Macedo, is also Portuguese.

Guilherme M. Luiz, a native of the Azores, founded the Portuguese newspaper, A Alvorada, in New Bedford, Massachusetts, which in 1920 became the Diário de Noticias. It was acquired in 1940 by João R. Rocha who published it until it expired in 1973.

1920   December 18. The Luzo Corporation of America, New Bedford, Massachusetts, a Portuguese loan bank, was chartered under the name of People's Loan and Property, Inc. On February 8, 1920, it had a paid up capital of $1,500, and by March 1, when it formally opened, had already made its first loan. The first president was Manuel E. Baptista. The other founders were António J. Medeiros, Manuel P. Rebello, Elias Barros Câmara, Alfredo J. Pacheco, and Francisco S. Mello. The bank started with an authorized capi-

tal of $20,000. This was increased to $250,000 in June, 1920.
In September, 1920, the board of directors was enlarged
from the original six members to twenty-five. From January 3, 1922, to January, 1936, Manuel L. Sylvia, the well-
known local capitalist, served as president. At the annual
meeting, 1925, the size of the board of directors was reduced from twenty-five to twenty. At a special meeting,
March 1, 1925, the chartered name of the bank was dropped
and its present name, Luzo Corporation of America, in
tribute to its Portuguese founders, was adopted instead. On
June 5, 1925, the bank's capital was increased to $750,000.
On January 1, 1926, a branch office was opened in Fall River. By 1930 there was another branch in North New Bedford.
The new building of the Luzo Corporation of America, at
the corner of River and Purchase streets, New Bedford was
formally dedicated on April 19, 1930. On Frebruary 11, 1945,
a banquet celebrating the bank's silver anniversary was
held in New Bedford. At that time the corporation was capi-
talized by the Portuguese, run and managed by them, and
its stockholders were restricted to people of Portuguese
origin or descent.

By 1920, about 15,000 first generation Azoreans and other
Portuguese accounted for a significant percentage of the
farms owned by foreign-born whites in California. As of
January, 1974, there were 63,000 farms in California, aver-
aging 573 acres in size.

The Portuguese of Fall River, Massachusetts, entered the
political arena for the first time. Only 7 percent of the
foreign-born Portuguese were naturalized American citizens.
By 1930, the percentage has risent to 12. In 1926, Attorney
Francis J. Carreiro was elected to the School Committee
and in 1930 John R. Machado to the city council. Machado,
who served for ten years as president of the Fall River Central Labor Union, was reelected to the council in 1932 and
again in 1934. By the middle of the 1940s, the majority of
the Portuguese in the city had become naturalized.

October 10. The Oakland Tribune published editorial com-
ment on the proposed monument in honor of the Portuguese
discoverer of California. "The decision to build a monument
to Cabrillo as the discoverer of California comes as the
culmination of years of effort in that direction on the part of
Jesse H. Woods, former Hayward merchant and capitalist
now a resident of Piedmont." Woods, the son of Portuguese

parents, began his efforts in 1903-1904, the year he served as the eleventh supreme president of the União Portuguesa do Estado da Califórnia (U.P.E.C.).

1920-1960   Sixty-five percent of the dairy farmers of California were Portuguese. Portuguese dairymen were instrumental in the development of cooperative creameries. In 1974 second and third generation Azoreans still served on the boards of directors of many of the creameries. They were also involved with Marin-Dell Creamery of San Francisco, which was sold to Foremost Dairies in the late 1950s.

c. 1920   The Portuguese ranked third in the ownership of land in California and fourth in the value of farms.

Two Holy Ghost festivals were given by the Portuguese people of the San Diego area, one in Point Loma and one in San Diego proper. The town celebration came to an end in 1963 but the original Point Loma festival continues. Following the discontinuance of the San Diego _festa_, the first crown of the Holy Ghost of the San Diego group was placed in a chapel built by Lawrence Oliver in the church of the University of San Diego, where it remains to this day.

1921   At a time when there were only about sixteen Portuguese families in La Playa and eight in Roseville, a group of Portuguese men from Pointa Loma, on San Diego bay, met at the home of Manuel de Oliveira Medina to propose the creation of a society whose main purpose would be to celebrate the annual festival in honor of the Holy Ghost, the third person of the Trinity, a traditional religious devotion of the Atlantic islanders. At another meeting, the organization was given the name that it still has, United Portuguese S|ocie-dade]. E [spírito]. S[anto]. Hall. Medina and Joe S. Rogers were elected president and secretary-treasurer, respectively. It was then decided that thenceforth every Portuguese-owned fishing boat would donate 25 cents for each ton of fish caught to a church fund and another 25 cents to a hall construction fund. Thanks to a loan from Rogers, a lot was purchased and the construction of the festival hall begun, on its present site in Roseville. The hall was finished in time for the 1922 _festa_ of the Holy Ghost. In 1947, the hall having outlived its usefulness, the board of directors, at M.O. Medina's instigation, voted to build a new one. The new hall, occupying almost a block in the heart of Point Loma, was finished in time for the Holy Ghost festival of 1948. The mortgage on it was fully paid in 1955. On March 10, 1973, the members of the United Portuguese S.E.S. Hall honored Medina, the man who in the intervening fifty years had served as their president, with a testimonial banquet, at which time the history of the society was outlined by Mário T. Ribeiro of San Diego, a Portuguese stock broker and investment counselor, and the career of the guest of honor was told, in the keynote address. The Portuguese Hall, as it is affectionately known, remains as a veritable community center for the Portuguese and Portuguese-Americans of San Diego, and it stands as a tribute to the foresight of the early pioneers who faced a problem with the conviction of those determined to do something about it.

1922   The bulletin of the Associated Milk Producers, edited by Mário Bettencourt da Câmara, appeared in San Francisco. It was intended for Portuguese dairymen.

The first Portuguese-language broadcast in the United States was over Station WDAU, New Bedford, Massachusetts. Alberto Corrêa was responsible for it.

The Grémio Lusitano was founded in Ludlow, Massachusetts.

The University of California Press published Sonnets and poems of Anthero de Quental, the celebrated man of letters from São Miguel, Azores, translated by S. Griswold Morley. Dr. Morley was for many years the chairman of the Department of Spanish and Portuguese at Berkeley.

Elsie Spicer Eells is the author of The Islands of Magic -- Legends, Folk and Fairy Tales from the Azores (New York: Harcourt, Brace and Company).

There are thirty obviously Portuguese names and a few mangled Portuguese names (such as Cardoza and Mederios) in Eugene T. Sawyer's History of Santa Clara county California with Biographical Sketches of the Leading Men and Women of the County Who Have Been Identified With Its Growth and Development From the Early Days to the Present (Los Angeles: Historical Record Company). Among the Portuguese listed (with their place and date of birth in parentheses) are the following: John Castelo (São Jorge, Azores, November 20, 1876), M. T. Sequeira (Faial, Azores, April 2, 1862), Manuel Bronk (San Luis Obispo, March 22, 1894), André Azevedo (São Jorge, January 19, 1874), Frank Silveira Corrêa

(Faial, February 19, 1881), Frank P. Alvernaz (Faial, December 25, 1873), Frank R. Machado (Terceira, Azores, 1866), John R. Freitas (Madeira, January 15, 1877), Domingos A. Silva (Pico, Azores, 1863), Manuel F. George (Half Moon Bay, August 21, 1868), Manuel S. Brazil (São Jorge, c. 1869), and Manuel T. Freitas.

André Azevedo, born in São Jorge, Azores, January 10, 1874, was a dairyman of Santa Clara county whose Vendome Ranch was one of the show places of Northern California. He came to the United States at the age of seventeen and to the Santa Clara valley in 1919. A member of the Portuguese Church of the Five Wounds of San Jose, he was one of the organizers of the Bank of Novato and served for many years on it board of directors. He was a charter member of the Milk Porducers Association, San Francisco, and for four years was a member of its board of directors. He was also a member of the Portuguese benevolent association, Irmandade do Divino Espírito Santo (I.D.E.S.).

1922-1925   O Cosmopolitano, a Portuguese monthly literary magazine, was published in Fairhaven, Massachusetts.

Eduardo de Carvalho was consul of Portugal in Boston. Under the pseudonym of Gil de Alverca he published Problemas da nossa colónia (Boston, 1924) and Palestras coloniais (Boston, 1924). Under the pseudonym of Caturrinha Colonial, in the same place and year, he published Falar e escrever.

1923   The American Tunaboat Association (ATA), with a membership comprised exclusively of American tunaboat owners, was organized in San Diego. The offices are at 1 Tunaboat Lane. In 1923 the industry was still in its infancy, but its beginnings were in San Diego, through the efforts of such Portuguese men of the sea as M.O. Medina, Joe S. Rogers, and Mathew C. Monise. Support for the ATA has come largely from Portuguese shipowners, and this support has enabled it to live and service its clientele. M.O. Medina, the man credited with starting the tuna fish industry in San Diego, served as president in 1950. In 1970-1973, the ATA collected about $5,000,000 in fines, licenses, port charges, and lost fishing time for its members.

1924   The Associação Beneficente Aliança Portuguesa (Portuguese Alliance Benevolent Association, Inc.), with offices at 570 South Main Street, Fall River, Massachusetts, began in 1920

CHRONOLOGY   65

but it was incorporated in 1924. It is the youngest of the
beneficent societies of Fall River and has about 4,000 members. (The other Portuguese societies of the city include
São José, Açoreana, São Miguel Arcanjo, Nossa Senhora
da Luz, and Monte Pio.) The first president was João Cabral; the secretary, Alberto Freitas, a native of Madeira
who came to the United States in 1912 and later joined the
editorial staff of the Diário de Notícias, New Bedford, Massachusetts, a connection that lasted fifty years. With the
reorganization of the Portuguese Alliance in 1934, Freitas
became president, a position that he has held to the present
time. In 1973, its assets amounted to $329,622.11. On
October 4, 1974, it celebrated its golden anniversary.

The first final examinations for proficiency in the Portuguese
language were held at the Ateneu Nacional Português (National Portuguese Athenaeum), Fall River, Massachusetts,
under the supervision of the Ministry of National Education,
Lisbon. The classes were taught by Mr. and Mrs. Manuel
de Sá Couto.

In 1924 Fall River was a great center of Portuguese activity,
with seven national Catholic parishes, five benevolent associations, four banks, three Portuguese-language newspapers, and dozens of clubs.

Alfredo Gomes and then António da Conceição Teixeira published A Abelha, a Portuguese journal of humor, first in
San Francisco and later in Oakland.

March 18. The first issue of A Colónia Portuguesa, a bi-
weekly Portuguese newspaper and the successor to O Lavrador Português, appeared on this day. The editor was Artur
V. Ávila, and Dr. Abílio Reis and Alberto Moura wrote for
it. It appeared until June 24, 1932, when it was merged with
other newspapers to form the Jornal Português of Oakland,
California.

Issac Goldberg is the author of Camoens: Central Figure
of Portuguese Literature, 1524-1580 (Girard, Kansas: Hal-
deman-Julius).

1925   A Portuguese grammar, by E.C. Hills, of the University
              of California; J.D.M. Ford, of Harvard University; and J.
              de Siqueira Coutinho, of The Catholic University of America,
              was published. It remained the standard grammar of the

language until the time of the Good Neighbor Policy when
Anglo-Americans, ignoring the psychological needs of the
large Portuguese community in the United States, demanded
grammars that stressed Brazil, not Portugal.

Founded in October, 1925, and incorporated on April 23, 1926,
the União Portuguesa Beneficente, Inc. (Portuguese Beneficent
Union), of 239 Central Avenue, Pawtucket, Rhode Island, is
a mutual aid society designed to assist members and their
families in sickness and in death. Membership is open to
persons of Portuguese descent or linked by marriage to such
persons, without regard for color, religion, or provenance.
The work of the organization is conducted in Portuguese.
There are several branches; the membership totals 1,200.
Resources are over $350,000.

November 1. A group of Portuguese immigrants from Portugal proper -- they are known as "continentals" in Portuguese-American circles -- founded the União Portuguesa
Continental dos Estados Unidos a América (Portuguese Continental Union of the United States of America). Organized
as a beneficent society for Portuguese continentals (as op-
posed to Portuguese from the Atlantic islands), it was incorporated under the laws of the Commonwealth of Massachusetts on October 1, 1929. The headquarters are at 899
Boylston Street, Boston. As of 1974, there are sixty-seven
lodges in Massachusetts, Connecticut, Rhode Island, New
York, New Jersey, Pennsylvania, New Hampshire, and Ontario,
(Canada). Today, membership is open to Portuguese of any
provenance, Luso-Americans, Luso-Canadians, Brazilians,
and others who by virtue of family or other ties are connected with the Portuguese community. There are no racial
or religious qualifications. As of January 1, 1970, the assets
of the union amounted to $1,468,737.09.

1926   A Crónica Portuguesa, A Portuguese newspaper edited by
Mário Bettencourt da Câmara, appeared in San Leandro,
California. Only two numbers were issued.

Stanford University published John Casper Branner's translation of Alexandre Herculano's History of the Origin and
Establishment of the Inquisition in Portugal. The Herculano
book -- the author was a noted Portuguese Liberal historian
-- played up to Anglo-Saxon prejudices on the Inquisition.

Dom António Augusto de Castro Meireles, bishop of the

Azores, who had come to the United States to attend the International Eucharistic Congress in Chicago, visited the important Portuguese centers of the United States.

The Portuguese American Civic League of Fall River, Massachusetts, was founded by Attorney Francis J. Carreiro, who was its first president.

The monthly magazine, Portugal-América, was published in Cambridge, Massachusetts, 1926-1929.

1927   O Facho of Hilo, the last of the Hawaiian Portuguese newspapers, came to an end.

The East Oakland, California, mission of the Portuguese Church of St. Joseph was erected into an independent parish under the invocation of Mary Auxilium Christianorum.

Eduardo Mayone Dias was born in Lisbon. In 1956 he took part in the International Teachers' Program, with classes at the American University, Washington, D.C. In 1971 he received the Ph.D. degree in Spanish from the University of Southern California, with a dissertation on Menéndez y Pelayo and Portuguese literature soon to appear in Biblos, of the University of Coimbra. He has written for a number of Portuguese reviews, including Seara Nova (Lisbon) and the Jornal Português (Oakland, California). At UCLA he is president of the Cabrillo Cultural Institute, an organization that has concerned itself with the records of the Portuguese presence in California. He is the author, along with Thomas A. Lathrop and Joseph G. Rosa, of a trial edition of Portugal: Língua e Cultura, a grammar of the Portuguese language which emphasizes European Portuguese (1974).

1928   A grammar of the Portuguese language, by Joseph Dunn, professor of Celtic at The Catholic University of America, was published by the Hispanic Society of America, New York. Another edition of the work appeared later in London. The Dunn grammar is the best reference grammar of the language to have appeared in a foreign country.

The Portuguese-American bilingual newsweekly Luso Americano was founded in Newark, New Jersey. The publisher is Vasco S. Jardim, a native of Madeira; the editor, Fernando Augusto dos Santos; the managing editor, António S. Martinho. On October 1, 1974, the newspaper had a circulation of 7,300 copies. Local correspondents cover happenings of interest to the Portuguese community, in Danbury, Hartford, New Haven, and Waterbury, Connecticut; Chicopee, Ludlow, New Bedford, and Taunton, Massachusetts; Elizabeth, New Jersey; Oakland, California; Bethlehem, Pennsylvania; Mineola and Tarrytown, New York; Lisbon, Ílhavo, and Murtosa, Portugal; and the Azores.

The Fernando Palha Portuguese collection of about 6,700 volumes and manuscripts was given to the Harvard College Library by John B. Stetson, Jr. A catalogue of the collection was published in 1896. By 1974, the Portuguese holdings, in history and literature, of the Harvard College Library have grown to 20,000 volumes.

December 27. António Alberto Costa, the radio-television personality and newspaper publisher, was born in Lisbon, Portugal. Educated in Lisbon and, after he had emigrated to the United States in 1948, in New Bedford, Massachusetts, he became an announcer-producer of Portuguese radio programs in New Bedford, Fall River, and Wickford (Rhode Island) over stations WBSM-AM, WALE-AM and FM, WKFD-AM, and WGGY-FM. In 1968-1970 he was the commentator-producer of the first telephone talk show in Portuguese in the United States. Since February, 1970, he has been the producer-host of "Passport to Portugal" on WTEV, channel 6, New Bedford-Providence (Rhode Island), with reruns in 1971-1973 over KMPH-TV of Visalia, California. He is the president-publisher of Portuguese Times, a weekly Portuguese language newspaper of Newark, New Jersey, which also maintains an office in New Bedford. He received an official citation from the Massachusetts House of Representatives, 1972, for his work on behalf of the Portuguese-American community; a commandery in the Order of Prince Henry the Navigator, from the Portuguese government, 1972; and the Prince Henry the Navigator Cross, Man-of-the-Year Award, from the Prince Henry Club of Rhode Island, 1973

1930   O Portugal, a weekly Portuguese newspaper published irregularly by João Roldão, made its appearance in Oakland, California. It was oriented towards the União Portuguesa Continenatl (U.P.C.) and immigrants from Ílhavo, Portugal.

July 26. The Irmandade de Santa Maria Madalena (Confraternity of St. Mary Magdalene) was founded in Oakland, Continental

The Rev. A.V. Soares (1860-1930) was pastor for many
years of a Portuguese Protestant church in Honolulu. Another Portuguese Protestant congregation existed in Hilo,
in charge of the Rev. Ernest G. de Silva (c. 1874-1955).

Joaquim Francisco de Freitas (1872-1940) published in Honolulu his Portuguese-American Memories, the best-known
book dealing with the Portuguese in Hawaii. Part of it is in
Portuguese.

According to the U.S. Census, there were 167,891 Portuguese of foreign white stock in the United States and an additional 27,588 (or 7.5 percent of the territorial population)
in Hawaii. Of the mainland Portuguese, 40 percent were
in California, the remainder essentially in New England.
Altogether there were 350,000 persons born in Portuguese
territory or with one Portuguese forbear.

Joaquim Joe Cardoso, known professionally as Jack J. or
J.J. Cardoso, was born in Mahoning Township, Pennsylvania,
on August 20. He has published several studies on the
American black and on the black experience.

There were 11,621 Portuguese in San Leandro, California.

Eleven police officers and five firemen of Fall River, Massachusetts, were of Portuguese descent. By 1959, the number
had risen to sixty-nine and fifty-three, respectively.

Gilberto S. Marques published Pedra de Dighton in New
York. It is part of the growing Portuguese literature on
Dighton Rock.

1931   Artur V. Ávila, the pioneer newspaperman of California,
a native of Pico, Azores, founded the first daily Portuguese
radio program in the Golden State over Station KTAB, Oakland.

J.D.M. Ford and L.G. Moffatt edited and published the
Letters of John III, King of Portugal. In 1933 they published
their edition of the Letters of the Court of John III King of
Portugal, with the Portuguese text and an introduction. In
1936, Ford published the hitherto unpublished Crónica de
Dom João de Castro by Leonardo Nunes. All the manuscripts
are from Harvard University's famous Fernando Palha Collection.

1932   February 2. A group of San Francisco and San Mateo members of the Associação Portuguesa Protectora e Beneficente (A.P.P.B) met at the home of Frank V. Seamas on Turk Street, San Francisco, to form the Dom Nuno Club, a Portuguese civic organization. In 1934 the name of the club was changed to Cabrillo Civic Club, in honor of the Portuguese discoverer of California. In 1974 there are Cabrillo Civic Clubs throughout California, and the main offices are at 1164 34th Avenue, Sacramento. Frank Nordeste is the executive secretary of the organization.

April. Forty thousand people from all over California converged on Oakland to celebrate the seventh centennial of the death of St. Anthony of Lisbon, also known as St. Anthony of Padua, the most famous of the Portuguese saints, and also to celebrate the fifth centennial of the discovery of the Azores. The festivities were organized by the supreme council of the União Portuguesa do Estado da Califórnia (U.P.E.C.) of San Leandro.

Porfírio Bessone is the author of Dicionário cronológico dos Açores, composed and printed by him in Cambridge, Massachusetts, to commemorate the fifth centennial of the Azores by Gonçalo Velho Cabral.

The Portuguese-American Club of Gustine, California, was begun in this year to encourage a civic spirit on the part of its members. In pursuit of this ideal, the club organized an annual week-long festival, beginning on September 8, dedicated to Our Lady of the Miracles. John T. Mattos was responsible for the first festival, popularly known as the Festa da Serreta, after its namesake in Terceira, Azores, and all subsequent ones, until his reitrement in 1947. During the festival, Gustine plays host to the gathering of the clans.

For the year ending June 30, 1932, 60 percent of the Hawaiian brides married outside of their own ethnic group, 45 percent of the Portuguese, and less than 5 percent of the Japanese.

Ferreira Martins was the author of Os portugueses em New Bedford: o 5º centenário dos Açores em New Bedford -- um século de actividade lusa na cidade -- o 50º aniversário do Montepio Luso-Americano 1432-1932 (The Portuguese in New Bedford; the fifth centennial of the Azores in New Bedford -- a century of Portuguese activity in the city -- the fiftieth anniversary of the Montepio Luso-Americano 1432-1932), published in New Bedford, Massachusetts.

1933   Alfredo Silva began to publish O Progresso, a Portuguese newspaper, in Sacramento, California. It ceased publication in 1940.

The Rev. J.J. Vieira, Jr., pastor of the Portuguese Methodist Church, Oakland, California, founded O Heraldo, a Portuguese newspaper, as a house organ.

A Portuguese literary review, Portugalia, was founded in Oakland by Dr. Joaquim R. da Silva Leite. It lasted for a few months.

Constantino de Barcelos began to publish As Novidades, a Portuguese newspaper, in Newman, California, but the publication was suspended a few months later.

1934   Two Portuguese periodicals were founded in Oakland, California, to serve as printed arms of two Portuguese radio programs, i.e. the Ecos de Portugal and O Clarim. The latter was published by Artur V. Ávila. In 1936, the two periodicals were merged under the name of Ecos de Portugal.

The Portuguese Church of St. Agnes was opened in Point Loma, on San Diego Bay. The pastor was the Rev. Manuel Francisco Rosa, born in San Leandro, California, of Portuguese parents.

1935   Monsignor Joseph Cacella, a Portuguese-American priest of the Archdiocese of New York, founded A Luta, "the Portuguese newspaper in the Empire State," a bi-weekly. The newspaper is the official organ of the Message of Fátima in the United States.

September 26 was Portuguese Day at the California Pacific Exposition, San Diego. The San Diego Portuguese community organized and maintained the House of Portugal (in the House of Pacific Relations) during the period of the fair, 1935-1936.

September 12. Dr. João de Bianchi, the minister of Portugal in Washington, D.C., on his visit to California, paid a courtesy call on the Portuguese Church of St. Joseph, Oakland. He also visited Stanford University, where he was received by former President and Mrs. Herbert Hoover at their hilltop residence overlooking the Quad. The Stanford visit was arranged by Manoel da Silveira Cardozo, from San Bernardino, California.

Joaquim António da Silveira, a native of Ribeira da Areia, São Jorge, Azores, who at one time enjoyed the reputation of being the richest Portuguese in the United States, was decorated by the Portuguese government with a knighthood in the Order of Christ. He emigrated to California at the age of seventeen and began to work as a farm hand on a dairy ranch. He then moved to Nevada, where he spent four years as a cowboy. He returned to California and in Vallejo went into dairying. He was destined to find his gold mine in the milk business. In 1905 he and other wealthy Portuguese founded the Portuguese-American Bank of San Francisco.

1936

Through the efforts of José Silva, the Portuguese language began to be taught at the B.M.C. Durfee High School, Fall River, Massachusetts. The teacher in charge was António Serpa. At the same time, Dr. Joaquim R. da Silva Leite, a prominent member of the Portuguese community of California, began to teach Portuguese in one of the high schools of Oakland.

June 30. According to the Bureau of Vital Statistics of the Territorial Board of Health, there were 29,863 Portuguese in Hawaii. Of these 28,109 were citizens; 1,754, aliens. The total population of the islands was 392,277.

The Portuguese-American League of San Diego, representing all the Portuguese-American organizations in the city, was organized as an outgrowth of local Portuguese involvement in the California Pacific Exposition (1935-1936).

Dom Manuel Gonçalves Cerejeira, Cardinal Patriarch of Lisbon, visited California at the invitation of the Supreme Council of the Sociedade Portuguesa Rainha Santa Isabel (S.P.R.S.I.) to take part in festivities, sponsored by the society, honoring the sixth centenary of the death of its patron, St. Elizabeth, Queen of Portugal (1271-1336).

1937

"Of the 79,974 white Portuguese (which excludes the 'Bravas' from the Cape Verde Islands), who were not born in this country, 24,840 are in Massachusetts, 22,695 in California, 8,118 in Rhode Island, 2,345 in Connecticut, 5,106 in New York, 3,655 in New Jersey, and 1,291 in Pennsylvania. The two largest colonies are in the region of New Bedford, Massachusetts, and Oakland, California. New Bedford has 5,294 residents who were born in Portugal, 6,992 from the Azores, and 1,509 colored 'Bravas' -- mostly from the Island of Brava in the Cape Verde group. Fall River is, of course, adjacent to New Bedford and it has 5,320 settlers who were born in Portugal, 4,392 from the Azores, and 71 'Bravas.' Oakland has 3,847 inhabitants who were born in Portugal, 637 from the Azores, and only 214 from the Cape Verde Archipelago." As so often happens with official American figures (Francis J. Brown and Joseph Slabery Roucek, eds., Our racial and national minorities: their history, contributions, and present problems, New York: Prentice-Hall, Inc., 1937), there is enormous confusion in designating the provenance of the Portuguese. Actually, both in Massachusetts as in California, the great majority are from the Azores.

The Cabrillo Civic Club of San Francisco officially unveiled a monument to João Rodrigues Cabrilho, the Portuguese discoverer of California, on San Miguel Island, off the Santa Barbara coast, on January 3, the anniversary of Cabrilho's death in 1543 on the same island. The idea for the memorial came from Dr. Joaquim R. da Silva Leite, the Grand Historian of the Cabrillo Clubs.

Vincent J. McNabb published St. Elizabeth of Portugal (New York: Sheed and Ward). To this medieval Portuguese queen, a princess of Aragon, are attributed the celebrated miracles of the roses.

Percy Alvin Martin, of Stanford University, a pioneer of Luso-Brazilian studies in the United States -- he was a close friend of, and greatly influenced by, Dr. Manoel de Oliveira Lima -- published "Portugal in America" in The Hispanic American Historical Review, XVII (1937), 182-210. The editor of the review for many years was Dr. James Alexander Robertson. Martin was well known among the leaders of the Portuguese community of the San Francisco bay area.

The Belle of Portugal, a San Diego tuna clipper 142 feet in length and capable of carrying 350 tons of fish was launched.

She was owned by a Portuguese consortium made up of Lawrence Oliver and the Garcia da Rosa brothers. The Belle
of Portugal was fishing ninety miles out of Panamá when she
caught fire and sank in January, 1967.

The Pioneer Civic Association, Honolulu, a Portuguese social and charitable organization with a membership of 150
that works with hospitals and provides food baskets for the
poor was founded. It also grants scholarships. The association was responsible for the statewide convention of Portuguese organizations that was held in July, 1973.

1938   Professor Edwin B. Williams, University of Pennsylvania,
published From Latin to Portuguese: Historical Phonology
and Morphology of the Portuguese Language (Philadelphia).
A number of doctoral dissertations in Portuguese were written under his direction.

Philip Goose, in his book St. Helena (London), referred to
an old saying that the directors of the East India Company
used to quote. "Where the English settle, they first build
a punch-house, the Dutch a fort and the Portuguese a church."

The Sociedade Portuguesa de Santo António Beneficente and
the Sociedade Lusitania Beneficente, with headquarters in
Hawaii, went out of business. These two beneficent societies had several hundred members in West Oakland, California.

William B. Greenlee translated and edited The Voyage of
Pedro Álvares Cabral to Brazil and India: from contempor-
ary Documents and Narratives (London: Hakluyt Society,
2d series, LXXXI). The late Mr. Greenlee, a student of
H. Morse Stephens, the pioneer Portuguese scholar of Cornell University and later of the University of California,
founded and endowed the celebrated Greenlee Collection of
Portuguese history in the Newberry Library, Chicago. One
of the great collections of its kind in the United States, it
reached its present excellence thanks in part to the efforts
of two librarians, Mrs. Ruth Lapham Butler and the late F.
Holden Hall.

Mabel Farnum is the author of a life of St. Francis Xavier,
the Narvarrese Apostle of the Missions in the service of
Portugal, A Carrack Sailed Away -- The Voyage of Master
Francis Xavier (Boston: The Society for the Propagation of

the Faith). She also wrote two other books on Portuguese saints, The Sacred Scimitar: Life of Blessed John de Brito, with an introduction by Manoel Cardozo (Milwaukee: The Bruce Publishing Company, 1946), and St. Anthony of Padua (New York: Didier, 1948).

1939   The regular teaching of the Portuguese language at the University of Hawaii began as the result of the concurrent resolution of the legislature of the Territory of Hawaii, introduced by the Portuguese-American representative, M.G. Paschoal, on March 13. Earlier, in 1925-1926, Professor Maro Beath Jones (1875-1945), of Pomona College, California, taught Portuguese at the Univeristy on a visiting basis.

There were the following Portuguese radio programs in California: "Voz dos Açores, " in Modesto and Visalia, under the direction of José Vitorino; "Castelos Romanticos, " Oakland, Artur V. Ávila; "Ecos de Portugal, " Oakland, Leonel Soares de Azevedo; "Voz de Portugal, " San Jose, Oakland, and Watsonville, Tomaz Dias; "Portuguese America, " Stockton, Manuel C. Leal; "Voz do Vale, " Modesto, J. Cabral; "Memórias de Portugal, " Sacramento, Gabriel Silveira; "Memórias de Portugal e Açores, " Merced, J.S. Marques; "Voz de Merced, " Merced, Betty Santos; "Ares Lusitanos, " Merced, George Costa; "As Cruzadas, " Merced, Raimundo Silva; "Memórias Internacionais, " Visalia, Anthony Souza; and "Cabrilho, " Monterey, Mrs. Soares de Azevedo.

Founding of the Associação Fraternal Luso-Americana (Portuguese-American Fraternal Association), a social and mutual aid society with headquarters at 214 Walnut Street, Newark, New Jersey.

May 20. The first regular transatlantic commercial air service began between New York and Lisbon, via Bermuda and the Azores.

The Portuguese controlled 75 percent of the cattle of the state of California, nearly 450,000 head, valued at over $30,000,000, with a yearly production of milk estimated at $24,000,000.

Gerald M. Moser, Pennsylvania State University, is the author of Les romantiques portugais et l'Allemagne (Paris: Jouve et Cie.). Dr. Moser has long concerned himself with Portuguese literature.

There were four Portuguese-surnamed members of the thirty-member House of Representatives, Territory of Hawaii: V.A. Carvalho and August Costa, Jr., from Hilo, Manuel G. Paschoal from Puunene, Maui; and Clem Gomes from Lihue, Kauai. The clerk of the House was also Portuguese surnamed, O.P. Soares, of Honolulu. Paschoal, Gomes, and Costa were chairmen of standing committees.

As late as 1939 the use of the Portuguese language was still compulsory in the meetings of the Portuguese beneficent societies of California. These then had a total of 42,000 members, reserve funds in excess of $5,000,000, bulletins with a joint circulation of 28,000 copies, over 500 centers throughout the state, and paid up benefits of $16,000,000.

1940   According to the U.S. Census, 63,062 immigrants from the Azores and Portugal lived in urban areas; 25,036, in rural. In California, the pattern was reversed: 11,707 lived in urban areas, 17,921 in rural.

June 30. The monument to Prince Henry the Navigator was unvelied in Fall River, Massachusetts. It was erected with money contributed by the Portuguese people of New England to commemorate the 800th anniversary of the Portuguese nation.

The August issue of The Hispanic American Historical Review, a publication of the Duke University Press, was devoted "to the history of the Portuguese world as a part of the centennial celebration of Portugal's eight centuries of existence." In a foreword, Dr. João de Bianchi, the Portuguese minister to the United States, said: "The Portuguese have been intimately associated with the Americas from the period of the discovery to the present. These associations have not been restricted to the southern continent alone; on the contrary they have included North America."

November 9. The Most Reverend Stephen Alencastre, titular bishop of Arabissus, died. He was born in Madeira on November 3, 1873, the sone of Lucio J. and Leopoldina Alencastre, and went to Honolulu in 1882. Alencastre was the first Portuguese bishop of the American Church.

December 15. The Portuguese-American Social and Civic Club of San Diego was founded, with approximately 125 members. Lawrence Oliver was the first president, M.O. Medina the first vice president, M.N. Frizado secretary, and Mrs. Minnie Cardozo treasurer. The meetings were conducted at first in Portuguese.

December 19. The statue of João Rodrigues Cabrilho was unveiled in San Diego. It was created by the Portuguese sculptor Álvaro de Bré and was a gift of the Portuguese government in 1936. A great tourist attraction, the monument is located on a magnificent prospect on Point Loma, overlooking the bay and ocean, owned and maintained by the National Park Service. The Cabrillo Museum adjoins it.

1941   Francis J. Bahia Corner of Little Compton, Rhode Island, is named after a Portuguese-American who was killed while serving in the Armed Forces during the Second World War.

December 7. The first Fall River, Massachusetts, hero in World War II, Charles Braga, Jr., perished when the U.S.S. Pennsylvania went down in Pearl Harbor. The great bridge over the Taunton River connecting Fall River and Somerset was named Braga Bridge in his honor at ceremonies on April 15, 1966.

The Hilo (Hawaii) Chamarrita Club, a social organization was founded. It was named after the celebrated square dance of the Azores.

Oakland had a Portuguese population of 12,000, the largest urban concentration of this ethnic group in California.

1942   June 14. The fiftieth anniversary of the founding of the Portuguese Church of St. Joseph, Oakland California was celebrated.

The fourth centennial of the discovery of California was commemorated by the Portuguese Library (Gabinete Português de Leitura) of Rio de Janeiro with an address by the noted Portuguese historian, Dr. Jaime Cortesão.

August 30. The first youth classes of the União Portuguesa do Estado da Califórnia (U.P.E.C.) were organized, with special insurance policies to cover the young members of the fraternal society.

1943   Charles E. Kany, of the University of California, and Fidelino de Figueiredo, the Portuguese man of letters who had earlier served as a visiting professor at Berkeley, published a series of booklets under the general title of Portuguese Conversation (Boston: D.C. Heath and Co.).

1944   Frank B. Oliveira, of Fall River, Massachusetts, the son of Azoreans from São Miguel, was elected to the State House as a representative (the first American of Portuguese ancestry to serve in that capacity). He held this position until his defeat in 1958.

Laurinda C. Andrade, together with João R. Rocha, editor and publisher of the Diário de Notícias, the Portuguese daily of New Bedford, Massachusetts, founded the Portuguese Educational Society of the same city. The purposes of the organization were "to promote the learning and teaching of the Portuguese language by granting scholarships to students who have successfully completed two years of High School Portuguese, to act as a center for dissemination of information, to promote cultural exchange between the three countries: The United States, Portugal, and Brazil (the largest and most populous of the Portuguese speaking countries)."

1945   The Portuguese-American Progressive Association, New York City, maintained the Luís Vaz de Camões School where Joaquim R. Peixoto taught Portuguese to the children of its members.

The Portuguese-American Citizens Club, New York City, was functioning in this year.

Mrs. Mary L. Fonseca, a Portuguese-American, joined the School Committee of Fall River, Massachusetts. Later she became a state senator, a post she has held for almost two decades.

1947   Ernesto Da Cal, of Queens College, New York, is the author of the article on Portuguese literature in the Columbia Dictionary of Modern European Literature (New York). Professor Da Cal, a native of Galicia, Spain, was instrumental in founding the Portuguese program at Queens, New York, and is recognized as an outstanding authority on Eça de Queiroz, the nineteenth-century Portuguese novelist whose works have been translated into English and published in England and in the United States.

1948   May 27. Machado Square in Fall River, Massachusetts, in

honor of the Portuguese-American John R. Machado, was
formally dedicated.

1949   November 5. Joaquim Esteves, a native of Altares, Ter-
            ceira, Azores, began his radio program, "O Portugal de
            Hoje, " over Station KLOK, San Jose, California. Esteves
            has also had two Portuguese television programs, one over
            channel 19 in Modesto and another over channel 11 in San
            Jose.

1950   Godfrey Ferreira Affonso, for many years a reporter for
            the Honolulu Advertiser, died. Born in Funchal, Madeira
            in 1875, he arrived in Hawaii in 1878.

            The American poet, Leonard Bacon, under the aegis of The
            Hispanic Society of America, New York City, published his
            translation of Os Lusiadas (1572) by Luís de Camões. Ba-
            con's The Lusiads of Luiz de Camões is the first American
            translation of the great Portuguese work and, according to
            some critics, the best English translation.

1951   Random House of New York City published Home is an
            Island, a sensitive and beautiful novelized autobiographical
            account of life on the island of Flores, Azores, by Alfred
            Lewis, the well-known Portuguese-American of Los Banos,
            California. Unlike most American and English accounts of
            the Azores, which are marred by nativistic prejudices that
            stem from egregious misunderstanding, the Lewis book is
            warm, human, and sympathetic.

1952   Admiral M.M. Sarmento Rodrigues, of the Portuguese Navy,
            was made an honorary citizen of Oakland, California. On
            another occasion, the same honor was accorded Paulo Cunha,
            the Portuguese minister of foreign affairs.

1953   Mary Gotaas, who taught for many years at a college in Vir-
            ginai, is the author of Bossuet and Vieira A Study in National,
            Epochal and Individual Style (Washington, D.C.: The Catho-
            lic University of America).

            In 1953, there were four Portuguese-Americans in the Ha-
            waiian House of Representatives; in 1969, two. A Portu-
            guese-American served in the Senate in the latter year.

1954   The honorary consul of Portugal in Honolulu since 1954,
            Frank Gomes Serrão, an American of Portuguese descent,

was born in Kaumana, Hilo, Hawaii, on March 7, 1912, the
son of Joseph G. and Emília Souza Serrão. For his contributions to the financial and political world he has been decorated by the governments of Spain and Portugal. As secretary of the Territorial Government, Serrão had occasion
to serve as acting governor.

1955   Manuel Madruga, Jr., son of the pioneer Portuguese family
of San Diego, ended his career as chief designer of ships
for the Campbell Machine Company of the same city. In
his day Madruga was one of the best designers and builders
of ships in Southern California. Some of the boats that he
built for the San Diego tuna fleet are still in service.

1956   The Portuguese were widely involved in various activities
in the San Joaquim Valley, California. They owned stores
and operated cattle-feed lots, engaging in milking. In land
ownership they exceeded their Danish competitors.

Clarence L. Azevedo, a Portuguese-American, was mayor
of Sacramento, California from 1956-1959. Richard H. Mar-
riott, whose mother is Portuguese, has been mayor since
1968.

1958   June. The Honorable August C. Taveira, a Portuguese-
American, became an associate justice of the Superior Court
of the Commonwealth of Massachusetts. Born on February
4, 1913, he is the son of Dr. and Mrs. Arthur J. Taveira,
both natives of Lisbon, Portugal.

There were seventeen Portuguese radio programs (some
cities had more than one) in the following California communities: Oakland, Tulare, San Jose, Modesto, Monterey,
Berkeley, Pacific Grove, San Rafael, Turlock, Merced, Palo
Alto, and Napa.

Public Law 85-892, of September 2, 1958, authorized non-
quota visas for Portuguese citizens who had been displaced
from their homes as the result of the volcanic eruptions
and earthquakes on the island of Faial, Azores in 1957. One
thousand, five hundred visas for heads of families (which
automatically included dependents) were initially authorized.
Public Law 86-648, of July 14, 1960, raised the number of
non-quota visas to 2,000 and extended the final date of issu-
ance from June 30, 1960, to June 30, 1962. A total of 4,811
Portuguese came to the United States under the Azorean

refugees acts. Under Public Law 87-301, of September 26, 1961, about 2,500 Portuguese were allowed to come to America.

1959   February 28. The Honorable Arthur A. Carrellas, the son of immigrants from São Miguel, Azores, was sworn in as associate justice of the Superior Court of the Commonwealth of Massachusetts. His parents, who owned a shoe store in Newport, Rhode Island, saw seven of their thirteen children receive college degrees.

1960   August Sousa Costa was living in retirement in San Leandro, California. He was a native of Angra do Heroísmo, Azores, 1887, and went to Hawaii about 1898. In Hawaii he served as county supervisor, 1903-1908, and worked on the Hawaii Herald, in Hilo. After moving to California, he wrote for O Reporter, a Portuguese newspaper of Oakland, and in time became president and manager of the Wailea Milling Company.

Voz de Portugal, a Portuguese newspaper, began to be published in Hayward, California. It continues to be owned and edited by Gilberto Lopes Aguiar. His son, Lourenço C. Aguiar began a companion monthly journal, of a humorour nature, O Companheiro da Alegria, in 1961.

There were 87,109 foreign-born persons in the United States who gave Portuguese as their native language, and 277,402 persons who declared that they were of Portuguese stock.

In 1960, 1,258 Portuguese aliens became naturalized citizens of the United States; in 1965, 1,718; in 1969, 1,543.

There were 32,000 Portuguese aliens in the United States. In 1965 there were 38,000; and in 1969, 72,000.

1961   President John F. Kennedy took note of an anniversary of the União Portuguesa do Estado da Califórnia (U.P.E.C.) in the following letter: "I want to extend my greetings to the Portuguese Union of the State of California and to all attending its seventy-fifth anniversary celebration August 5th in Oakland. I commend the U.P.E.C. for its seven and a half decades of work and congratulate it on having Chief Justice Earl Warren as a member. My very best wishes."

1962   Dr. Manoel Cardozo, ordinary professor of history and curator of the Oliveira Lima Library, The Catholic University of America, born in Ribeiras, Pico, Azores, on December 24, 1911, was elected president of the American Catholic Historical Association. His presidential address was entitled "The idea of history in the Portuguese chronicles of the Age of Discovery."

Joe A. Gonsalves, a member of a pioneer Southern California Portuguese dairy family, was elected to the California Assembly by a 270-vote majority. In 1970 and 1972 he received over 70 percent of the votes cast. He lost to his Republican opponent in 1974. At the time of his defeat he was chairman of the Assembly Committee on Revenue and Taxation. He served as chairman of the Assembly Rules Committee. Before going to Sacramento, he was on the Cerritos City Council from 1958-1962, and mayor of Cerritos, from 1961-1962. He was a presidential elector in 1964 and 1968.

May 14. Artur Vieira de Ávila, generally known as Artur V. Ávila, a native of Lajes, Pico, Azores, where he was born on March 5, 1888, died in Oakland, California. He emigrated to the United States in 1909, and in 1912 founded O Lavrador Português, the first Portuguese newspaper in the San Joaquim valley. Later he turned to radio and made a name for himself when he and his wife, Celeste Alice Santos, a native of Trás-os-Montes, Portugal, known professionally as Rosinha, organized and maintained Portuguese-language radio programs in the Oakland area. The "Castelos Românticos" (Romantic Castles) of Artur and Celeste Avila was the most famous Portuguese radio program of its day. On the eve of his death, Ávila published two books of Portuguese verse that he had written over the years for his radio programs, Desafio radiofónico and Rimas de Um Imigrante (Versos para a Rádio). Both were published in Oakland in 1961. Ávila had a sensitive poetic vein, a fine command of words, and his poetry must surely be the best that has been printed in the Portuguese language in the United States.

1963

June. The Açoreana band of Fall River, Massachusetts, celebrated its golden jubilee.

July 12. The Luso-American Educational Foundation, sponsored by the Luso-American Federation of San Francisco, was incorporated as a non-profit organization under the laws of the State of California. Its purpose was to spread Portu-

guese culture. With funds supplied largely by the United
National Insurance Society, San Francisco, the Foundation
has awarded scholarships for advanced study in Portuguese
and made grants to cultural and academic meetings of a
Portuguese nature. Since 1966, the Foundation has annually
celebrated June 10 as "Portuguese Day." In a special way,
it concerns itself with the teaching of Portuguese in the
schools of California.

1964   March 24. A statue by the Portuguese sculptor, Numídico
            Bessone Borges de Medeiros Amorim, dedicated "To the
            Portuguese immigrant," was unveiled in historic Root Park,
            San Leandro, California. The statue cost $5,250 and was
            paid for by members of the União Portuguesa do Estado da
            Califórnia (U. P. E. C.).

            July 5. The Portuguese-American Federation, with offices
            in East Providence, Rhode Island, bringing together about
            188 Portuguese civic, social, and fraternal organizations
            in New England, came into being, thanks to the efforts of Dr.
            Manuel Luciano da Silva, a well-known physician of Bristol,
            Rhode Island, and a leader of the Portuguese community of
            New England.

            The Right Reverend Monsignor António P. Vieira died. He
            was pastor of Mount Carmel Church, New Bedford, Massachu-
            setts, and a priest for seventy-five years. He was born in
            Feiteira de Achada, São Miguel, Azores, in 1866, and was
            ordained in 1888. He came to the United States in 1903. In
            1907 he became pastor of Mount Carmel. In 1941 he built
            the Mount Carmel Parochial School and in 1953, the Convent
            of the Sisters of Dorothy.

1965   August Mark Vaz, a Portuguese-American, is the author of
            The Portuguese in California, published by the Irmandade do
            Divino Espírito Santo (I. D. E. S.). It is the best work of its
            kind on the subject.

1966   The Immigration and Naturalization Act was implemented
            in 1966. This opened the doors to Portuguese immigration.
            Since 1965, 30,000 Portuguese have settled in Massachusetts.
            In 1969, 7,000 settled in Massachusetts and Rhode Island.

            Jean R. Longland, of the Hispanic Society of America, New
            York, published her Selections from contemporary Portu-
            guese poetry A Bilingual Selection (Irvington-on-Hudson,

New York: Harvey House, Inc.). There is a foreword by
Professor Ernesto Guerra Da Cal, of Queens College, New
York.

1967   The First Baptist Church, Fall River, Massachusetts, was re-
                ported as having hundreds of former Portuguese Catholics
                and their offspring in its congregation.

                John Vasconcellos, of the 24th Assembly District of Califor-
                nia, a lawyer of Portuguese ancestry, has been elected to
                the California legislature on the Democratic ticket since
                1967.

                After serving as supreme secretary of the Sociedade Portu-
                guesa Raínha Santa Isabel (S.P.R.S.I.), Oakland, California,
                for twenty-two consecutive years, Mrs. Leopoldina C. Rod-
                rigues Alves was retired.

1968   Laurinda C. Andrade, a native of São Braz, Terceira, Azores,
                where she was born on December 20, 1899, published her
                memoirs The Open Door in New Bedford, Massachusetts.
                The book is described as "the story of an immigrant Portu-
                guese in New Bedford, Massachusetts, who achieved outstand-
                ing success after passing through the local cotton mills, our
                public school system and Pembroke College, and who later
                founded the first high school Portuguese language department
                in the United States. Miss Andrade was chosen to head the
                Portuguese Department of New Bedford High School when it
                was created in 1955, the first such department in any Ameri-
                can high school, a position she held until her retirement.

1969   The Fundação Beneficente Faialense (Beneficent Foundation
                of Faial), was established, with headquarters in New Bed-
                ford, Massachusetts. There are branches in Bristol and
                East Providence, Rhode Island, In Horta, Faial, Azores, and
                in the Greater Boston Area. Its appeal is to the recent im-
                migrants from the island of Faial.

                Governor Ronald Reagan of California proclaimed March
                2-8 as Portuguese Immigrant Week, in honor of the "many
                citizens of the State of California ... of Portuguese descent"
                who have contributed "much to the growth and prosperity of
                the Golden State...."

                There is an independent Portuguese Baptist Church on Inman
                Street, Cambridge, Massachusetts, with a virtually all-Portu-

guese congregation of seventy members. It began in Boston
in 1900 as a Methodist congregation.

September 21-28. The Cabrillo Festival was part of the
program in connection with the second centennial of the
founding of San Diego (1769-1969).

1970   In June, radio station WGCY of New Bedford, Massachusetts,
became a full-time Portuguese language broadcaster. Other
New England stations with programs in Portuguese include
WLYN, WHIL, AND WUNR of Boston, and WNBM-FM of
New Bedford. WTEV (channel 6), New Bedford, presents a
weekly TV program in Portuguese as well as other programs
of a Portuguese nature.

One-third of the names in the Fall River, Massachusetts,
high school graduation list were Portuguese. Forty-five of
the 166 Fall River graduates of Southeastern Massachusetts
University were of Portuguese descent.

George Rogers, a Portuguese-American with an Anglicized
name, was mayor of New Bedford, Massachusetts from 1970
to 1971. He served at one time as a state representative
and in 1974 he was again on the city council.

The population of California amounted to 19,957,304. Of
this number, 62,857 were native born of Portuguese parentage and 17,805 were foreign-born Portuguese, or a total of
80,662 Portuguese. (There are many other Portuguese in
California not identified as such by the U.S. Census.)

The Right Reverend Monsignor John A. Silvia, a Portuguese-
American born in Fall River, Massachusetts, died. He was
pastor of the Church of St. John the Baptist, New Bedford,
Massachusetts. During his incumbency, the new St. John's
School was built in 1957.

1971   According to the manual of the school committee of the City
of New Bedford, Massachusetts, there were 281 Portuguese
surnamed persons on the payroll of the public school system.
There was a Portuguese-American on the school board, the
veteran Mrs. Rose Ferreira, first elected in 1952, seven
Portuguese surnamed school principals, and nine assistant
principals. The Portuguese language was offered in the New
Bedford High School and in the three junior high schools.

March 13. The U.P.E.C. Cultural Center was dedicated. It has headquarters of the União Portuguesa do Estado da Califórnia (U.P.E.C.) and of Council No. 1 (San Leandro) and the J.A. Freitas Library, with an auditorium and conference rooms, in San Leandro, California. The center is the first of its kind in California.

Eugenie Carneiro, a native of Shanghai and a descendent of Portuguese, died. For many years she was an official of the International Student House, Berkeley, California.

An organization whose membership is limited to children was founded in Honolulu. It is called Crianças de Portugal (Children of Portugal), and the purpose of the society is to teach Portuguese dances and the history and culture of the Portuguese who came to Hawaii to its members.

1972

April. José Fernandes, who was born 78 years ago on the island of Madeira, and was the founder of the Fernandes supermarket food chain, with offices in Norton, Massachusetts, died.

April 13. By motion of Councilman Manuel F. Neto, a Portuguese-American, New Bedford, Massachusetts, became the "sister city" of Horta, Faial, Azores. In the furtherance of this relationship, dignitaries of the two cities have exchanged visits and on one occasion the Horta soccer team came to New Bedford.

A club by the name of Passarinho de Portugal (Little Bird of Portugal), Honolulu, designed to teach its members Portuguese dances and the history and culture of the Portuguese, was founded.

Earl J. Dias, of Fairhaven, Massachusetts, of Portuguese parentage, was named chairman of the Department of English, Southeastern Massachusetts University. Since 1947 he has served as drama and music critic for the New Bedford Standard-Times. He has written several books and numerous articles.

1973

November 18. The new pavilion at Dighton Rock, on the Massachusetts coast near Fall River, was dedicated in the presence of 3,000 people. Thanks to a state grant, a cofferdam was erected to raise the Rock eleven feet above its original level.

José S. Silva, a native of Graciosa, Azores, was the first
president of the Portuguese Credit Union, Cambridge, Massachusetts, known as "the bank of the Portuguese in Greater
Boston." He is a former president of the Portuguese Cultural Society of Cambridge.

Augusto J. Andrade, who was born on São Miguel, Azores,
is the owner of the Pawtucket Braid Company, Pawtucket,
Rhode Island. He is also president of the Alliance Finance
Company, and takes an active part in the business life of
Rhode Island.

Rudolph A. da Silva, a Portuguese-American, was mayor
of Taunton, Massachusetts.

The Luso-American Soccer Association was organized in
New Bedford, Massachusetts.

Our Lady of Fátima Roman Catholic Church was founded as
a Portuguese parish in Elizabeth, New Jersey.

Sixty percent of savings deposits in Fall River banks and
other financial institutions belong to people of Portuguese
ancestry.

In Fall River, there are four dentists of Portuguese descent,
four physicians, and ten attorneys. The only Portuguese
medical examiner in the United States, Dr. Othilia P. Vieira,
lives in the city.

1974   John M. Arruda, a Portuguese-American who served for six
years as mayor of Fall River, Massachusetts (reportedly the
first Portuguese-American mayor of an American city), is
the executive director of the Fall River Housing Authority.

According to a survey conducted by the Brazilian Embassy
and the Brazilian-American Cultural Institute, Washington,
D.C., 113 American colleges and universities offer courses
in the Portuguese language.

There is a Portuguese honor society, Phi Lambda Beta.
There are also two other national organizations for the aca-
demic community, American Association of Teachers of
Spanish and Portuguese and the Society for Spanish and
Portuguese Historical Studies. The latter two are oriented
towards Spanish interests. The AATSP began as an associ-

ation of teachers of Spanish but enlarged its purview when Portuguese began to be taught on a national scale.

Governor Ronald Reagan of California signed a bill into law that will henceforth exempt Portuguese fraternal organizations from turning over unclaimed insurance funds to the state government, provided that these proceeds be placed in trust for scholarship aid to California residents of Portuguese descent.

Edmund Dinis, a prominent lawyer of New Bedford, Massachusetts, has served as a state representative (1949-50), state senator (1953-56), district attorney for the Southern Distric of Massachusetts (1959-70) -- he achieved notoriety at the time of the Chappaquiddick incident involving Senator Edward Kennedy -- and since 1973 as treasurer of Bristol county.

The Portuguese American Council of New Bedford, Massachusetts, sponsors a regular television program, "The Portuguese around us." António Alberto Costa, owner of the newspaper Portuguese Times, produces another Portuguese television program, "Passport to Portugal."

With the death of Chief Justice Earl Warren of the United States Supreme Court, Council No. 55, San Leandro, California, of the União Portuguesa do Estado da Califórnia (U.P.E.C.), lost its most distinguished member. Warren joined the Portuguese organization on August 29, 1925, when he was district attorney of Alameda County.

Portuguese cultural centers, both named after Cabrilho, the Portuguese discoverer of California, are in operation on the campuses of the University of California in Los Angeles and Berkeley.

The Library of the University of California at Los Angeles has a collection on Portugal and Portuguese Africa amounting to about 54,000 volumes. In 1964 UCLA acquired the library of Joseph Benoliel, consisting of some 8,000 books, periodicals, and manuscripts, and including the personal library and papers of Xavier da Cunha, director of the National Library, Lisbon, 1902-1910. In 1965 the University also acquired a portion of the library of the Duke of Palmela, of the Portuguese peerage, including approximately 1,500 volumes on Portuguese subjects. Portuguese language and literature are the responsibility of the University under the Farmington Plan, and a blanket order for publications in these fields was placed in 1964. Since 1966, the Library has added two extremely rare Portuguese incunabula, both of 1489. Materials on Portuguese Africa has been purchased with a grant from the Ford Foundation.

The Portuguese are the most rural of the national groups in California. More Portuguese are involved in agriculture than any other ethnic group. More than 50 percent of the California Portuguese live in the Central Coast area, 25 percent in Alameda County. All the California settlement areas are dominated by Portuguese from the Azores.

There are 1,468 herds owned by the Portuguese of California, with a total of 333,236 cows. Based on a value of $2,500 per cow, the Portuguese investment amounts to $833,090,000, or $567,000 per farm.

Seventy percent of the market milk producers of Tulare, Kings, and Merced counties, California, are Portuguese; in Stanislaus, Fresno, and Madera counties, 40 percent.

The Portuguese account for 34 percent of all market milk produced in California. The Dutch are in second place, with 24 percent.

The California Milk Producers Advisory Board of Modesto, representing the 2,464 milk producers of the state, has five Portuguese on its twenty-four man board of directors.

Seven of the thirteen directors of the California Manufacturing Milk Producers Advisory Board of Modesto are Portuguese. The board represents the 1,240 manufacturing milk producers of California.

Forty-five percent of the membership of Associated Dairymen, Lodi, California, a milk producers association, is Portuguese. The manager, Louis Barcellos, also is Portuguese, as are ten of the twenty-one directors. Membership is recruited from the northern end of the San Joaquim valley, the Sacramento valley, and the northern part of the San Francisco bay area.

Fifty percent of the membership of the Producers Market Milk Association of San Jose, California, is Portuguese. Three of the nine directors are also Portuguese.

The Western Dairymen's Association of Merced, California, is managed by a second-generation Portuguese, Joe Branco. Of the thirteen directors, eight are of Portuguese descent. Seventy percent of the membership is also Portuguese.

Harry Corea, a second-generation Portuguese, is manager of the Los Angeles Mutual Cooperative, of Montebello. Three of the seven directors are Portuguese.

Twenty percent of shippers of the Humboldt Creamery Association, Fernbridge, California, are Portuguese dairymen. Three of the fifteen directors are also Portuguese.

The membership of the East-West Dairymen's Association of Newman, California, is 75 percent Portuguese. Three of its six directors are Portuguese, as is Manuel Lemos, the Association's field representative.

The Portuguese comprise 35 percent of the membership of the California Cooperative Creamery, Petaluma. One of the nine directors is a third-generation Portuguese.

Four of the nine directors of the Challenge Foods Company, Los Angelese, a cooperative marketing the milk of thirteen individual cooperative units, eleven in California and two in Idaho, are Portuguese.

Glenn Milk Producers, Willows, California: four of the nine directors are Portuguese; membership is 25 percent Portuguese.

The president of the League of California Milk Producers, with headquarters in Sacramento, is a Portuguese, Albert Soares, of San Jose. Four of the twenty directors are also Portuguese. The organization is a statewide legislative association representing seven producer associations.

The Dairymen's Cooperative Association, Tulare, California, founded in 1919, is still controlled by the Portuguese. George de Medeiros, the manager, is a second-generation Portuguese. Of the seven members of the board of directors, five are second-generation Portuguese.

"Recordar é viver" (To remember is to live) is a Portuguese radio program heard over station KGOY, Santa Maria, California. The director of the program, Manuel A. Martins, also tapes programs for the Portuguese broadcast, "Perfume de Portugal, " of San Diego.

"Voz do Imigrante" (Voice of the Immigrant) is broadcast in Hartford, Connecticut, by Fernando Gonçalves, Sundays, 11 a.m. to 1 p.m.

Manuel Nunes is in charge of "A Voz Portuguesa de Ludlow" (The Portuguese Voice of Ludlow, Massachusetts), a radio program.

There are annual festivals dedicated to Our Lady of Fátima in Los Banos and Thornton, California.

There is a Peter Francisco Park, named after the Portuguese hero of the American Revolution in the Ironbound district of Newark, New Jersey. The Ironbound is heavily Portuguese.

County Commissioner Charles A. Frates died in New Bedford, Massachusetts at the age of 82. The political career of this Portuguese-American began in 1938 when he was elected common councilman for the fifth ward of New Bedford.

There is a reader in Portuguese, appointed by the Ministry of Education, Lisbon, at the University of California, Santa Barbara.

Belmira E. Tavares, the daughter of Azorean pioneers from São Miguel, Azores, who emigrated to the United States 1880, is the author of Portuguese pioneers in the United States.

The first drivers manual ever to be issued in the United States in the Portuguese language has been published by the Department of Motor Vehicles, Rhode Island. This is an indication of the number of recent immigrants. There are more Portuguese in Rhode Island in proportion to the total population than in any other state of the union.

A committee was organized to revive the traditional festival of the Holy Ghost in Little Compton, Rhode Island, on August 3, 1975, in connection with the township's 300th birthday celebration. The Portuguese held their first such festa at the turn of the century. In the 1920's a Holy Ghost Hall was built by the Portuguese people for their annual event. The practice was discontinued during the Second World War.

During the Nixon administration, Ernest Ladeira, of Fall River, Massachusetts, the son of parents born on São Miguel, Azores, was the most important official of the federal government of Portuguese descent. He served at one time as Mr. Nixon's special adviser on social welfare and also as an assistant to John Volpe, Secretary of Transportation.

Eduardo Mayone Dias believes that the number of Portuguese immigrants in California and thier first-generation American-born descendants has been exaggerated. According to his calculations, there are no more than 40,000 of the former, and at the most 150,000 of the latter. If his figures are correct, it is obvious that the Portuguese achievement in California is proportionately greater too.

There are about thirty Portuguese Roman Catholic parishes in New England in charge of some fifty Portuguese priests.

There are seven Portuguese Roman Catholic parishes in Rhode Island.

There are four Roman Catholic parishes in New Bedford, Massachusetts, that cater to the spiritual needs of the local Portuguese community: St. John the Baptist, Our Lady of Mount Carmel, Immaculate Conception, and Our Lady of the Assumption. The latter is particularly frequented by Cape Verdeans.

There are two Portuguese Protestant churches in Fall River, two in New Bedford, and one in Cambridge, Massachusetts.

The mayor of Middletown, Connecticut, is a Portuguese-American.

Half of the population of Bristol, Rhode Island, is made up of Portuguese and Portuguese-Americans. The mayor and sixteen other elected officials are Portuguese.

Our Lady of Light Society, a Portuguese benefit association of Fall River, Massachusetts, has a membership of 500. The society has both sick and death benefits.

March. The gymnasium-auditorium complex of St. Joachim's Church, Hayward, California, serving as a new community center, was completed at a cost of $340,676. The pastor, the Rev. Albano G. Oliveira is a Portuguese-American.

October 1. A new Portuguese radio program, "Portugal-Brasil, " began to be broadcast over station KBRO, San Francisco.

November. Registration day for a Portuguese class which the Board of Education of Harrison, New Jersey, bowing to public demand, agreed to sponsor.

1975   The Fado Restaurant, Acushnet, Massachusetts, featuring Portuguese cuisine and owned by Frank Rebelo, is the base of operations for his famous wife, known professionally as Valentina Félix, a native of Algarve, Portugal, America's most genuine fado singer.

TEXTS AND STUDIES

The following texts are transcriptions of illustrative documents from printed sources. The Studies are brief historical essays especially written for this volume. Both were chosen or composed for real or symbolic reasons.

Studies generally deal with themes or topics that do not lend themselves to the documentary form. The nature of the published materials on the Portuguese in the United States is such that any other approach would have necessarily given a more fragmentary view of the subject and been a disservice to the reader.

Texts and Studies are interspersed indiscriminately, without generic labelling, but they are grouped in obvious patterns. The provenance of each is indicated in the individual bibliographies.

The interpolation by the author of supplementary data in a document appears within brackets. Ellipsis marks are used for deletions.

THE PORTUGUESE PIONEERS IN PERSPECTIVE

Source: Jaime Cortesão, Os portugueses no
descobrimento dos Estados Unidos (Lisbon,
1949), pp. 63-64. Translation by the editor.

Do you think that this hunger for space that drove the Portuguese between 1540 and 1543 upon the coasts and across the heartland of the United
States was a sporadic thing, a casual happening that led them to that corner
of the globe? Not at all. At the same time, in the captaincies of Brazil,
João Ramalho and the other Portuguese left by Martin Afonso de Sousa had
already burst upon the hinterland of São Paulo; the companions of Tourinho
were leaving their base of operations in Porto Seguro to search for emer-
alds in the direction of the River São Francisco; the sons of Diogo Álvares,
Caramuru, were exploring the interior of Bahia; and Duarte Coelho, from
his captaincy of Pernambuco, was writing to the King urging him to continue
exploring the interior of the Brazilian Northeast, interrupted by the tragic
failure of João de Barros' expedition. In Africa, the great routes of pene-
tration to the plateaus of the interior, the Congo and the Zambesi, began
to be tenaciously gone over and marked. Farther away, from one end of
Asia to the other, while Estêvao Gomes crossed the Red Sea with his armada and in a challenge to the Turk, dubbed his horsemen knights on Mount
Sinai, the Portuguese had already founded the Portuguese city of Liamp in
China; and in that very year of 1542, Fernão Mendes Pinto and his companions discovered Japan, and introduced firearms to the astonished Japanese.
. . .
Thus, while João Rodrigues Cabrilho was exploring the hitherto unknown
coast of California, in the unknown Far West, other Portuguese were dis-
coverning the farthest reaches of the Far East of the planet.

THE DISCOVERER OF CALIFORNIA

California Senate Concurring Resolution

Source: Senate Concurrent Resolution, no. 15.
Introduced by Senator McGovern. Sacramento,
January 23, 1935.

Whereas, Jaun [sic] Rodriguez Cabrillo, a native of Portugal, discovered California on Thursday, September 28, 1542, while in the service
of the King of Spain by entering the harbor of San Diego; and
Whereas, The discovery of California by Cabrillo was an event of
world-wide importance, and the anniversary of such event is of particular
interest to the people of the State of California; now, therefore, be it
Resolved by the Senate, the Assembly concurring, as follows:
That the people of the State of California are called upon to observe "Cabrillo Day" on the twenty-eighth day of September of each year by appropriate patriotic observances, and the Governor of the State of California is
hereby requested to issue a proclamation to the people of this State, each
year, calling their attention to the anniversary of the discovery of California by Jaun Rodriguez Cabrillo.

FOLK HERO OF THE AMERICAN REVOLUTION

Source: Nomination of "Peter Francisco
House" for the National Register of Historical Places by the Virginia Historic Land-
marks Commission, Richmond, March 16,
1972; Notes on Virginia, published by the
same Commission, fall of 1974; certified
copies of the pertinent proclamations.

The national origins of Peter Francisco, the only folk hero of the American Revolution, are clouded in mystery, but he seems to have been born in
Portugal or even on one of the Portuguese Atlantic islands. When he was
found, alone and forsaken, on the wharf at Hopewell, Virginia, the well-
dressed child, who may have reached America on a slaver or one one of
the ships that regularly sailed between Virginia and Portuguese ports, spoke
a language that the local people identified as Portuguese. He has since been
regarded as Portuguese.

At the age of 5 or 6, Judge Anthony Winston found the lad abandoned in
Prince George County and brought him home to Hunting Towers, where he
raised him. In 1776, at 16, the young man enlisted in a revolutionary regiment and fought in the northern battles of Brandywine, Germantown, Mon-
mouth, Stony Point, and Paulus Hook. Later he took part in the southern
campaign against Cornwallis. At Guilford Courthouse, he is reputed to have
slain 11 British soldiers, and at Camden, salvaged a 1,100 pound cannon
by sheer brute strength. A well-known painting of the remarkable Peter
Francisco, who was held in high regard by General Washington himself,
records the skirmish with Lord Tarleton's men.

Pensioned after the war, he worked as a blacksmith in Buckingham
County, where a grateful Virginia gave him 200 acres of land. Here he
guilt "Locust Grove," popularly known as "Peter Francisco House," his
place of residence from 1794 to the mid-1820's. At the time of his death
on January 16, 1831, he was the revered sergeant-at-arms of the Virginia
House of Delegates. The Assembly voted a resolution of regret at his pass-
ing and the funeral was conducted in the State Capitol, with burial in a famous Richmond cemetery, alongside other revolutionary notables.

A 99-year lease on "Locust Grove," now in ruins, has been negotiated
with Willard Spencer, the owner, by the Society of the Descendants of Peter
Francisco, which plans to restore and preserve it for posterity.

Massachusetts and Rhode Island both celebrate Peter Francisco Day,
the former since 1954, the latter since 1955 (as may be seen from the state
proclamations reproduced below). The Portuguese Continental Union of the

United States of America bestows its Peter Francisco Award upon
distinguished Americans who have contributed to the Portuguese cause.

The Commonwealth of Massachusetts

By His Excellency

FRANCIS W. SARGENT
Governor

A PROCLAMATION
1974

WHEREAS, Peter Francisco, a boy of Portuguese origin, at the age of
sixteen enlisted in the Continental Army so that his country might be free
from tyranny; and
WHEREAS, His outstanding qualities of courage and fortitude as well
as his staunch patriotism earned him great respect and gratitude from General George Washington; and
WHEREAS, It is said that Peter Francisco killed eleven men in one
battle and on another occasion captured an enemy cannon without assistance
and turned its fire upon the retreating foe; and
WHEREAS, After the war of freedom, he remained in service to his
country as Sergeant-at-Arms of the House of Delegates in his State of Virginia and continued his active support of the rights and freedoms of the
weak and unprotected;
NOW therefore, I, FRANCIS W. SARGENT, Governor of the Commonwealth of Massachusetts, in accordance with Chapter 124 of the Acts of
1954, do hereby proclaim as
PETER FRANCISCO DAY
March 15, 1974
and urge the citizens of the Commonwealth to take cognizance of this event
with suitable ceremonies in our schools and in other public assemblies, in
tribute to this great American patriot of Portuguese descent.
GIVEN at the Executive Chamber in Boston,
this seventeenth day of December, in the
year of our Lord, one thousand nine hundred
and seventy-three, and of the Independence
of the United States of America, the one
hundred and ninety-eighth.
FRANCIS W. SARGENT.

PROCLAMATION
PETER FRANCISCO DAY

By Dennis J. Roberts
Governor

Stirring words are to be found upon a monument at the battlegrounds of Guilford Courthouse, North Carolina. They tell of the climatic event in the life of a heroic young man, of Portuguese origin, PETER FRANCISCO.

The inscription reads: "To Peter Francisco, a giant in structure, might and courage, who slew in this engagement eleven of the enemy with his own broadsword, rendering himself, thereby, perhaps the most famous private soldier of the Revolutionary War."

At an early age Peter Francisco came to Virginia. When the Revolution came, he was sixteen years of age. He joined the Tenth Virginia Regiment of Continental troops and was engaged in some of the war's most sanguinary conflicts until victory was achieved. Rarely have his feats of heroism and daring been equalled in American history. He was completely dedicated to the ideals of freedom and democracy. As a result naturally he was wounded several times in the endeavor to secure liberty for the newly-born American Republic.

Later in life, Peter Francisco, who was industrious, temperate and always devoted to the cause of the weak and unprotected, became Sergeant-at-Arms of the House of Delegates in Virginia. He died in this public service on January 16, 1836 |sic|, and received burial with military honors.

On this historic anniversary which honors a truly great American of Portuguese origin; NOW, THEREFORE, DO I, DENNIS J. ROBERTS, GOVERNOR OF THE STATE OF RHODE ISLAND AND PROVIDENCE PLANTATIONS, PROCLAIM

TUESDAY, MARCH 15TH, 1955, AS
PETER FRANCISCO DAY,

urging that the occasion be marked by suitable ceremonies in our schools and other public assemblies, since truly it may be said that by the arms of such men the liberty of our Country was achieved.

IN TESTIMONY WHEREOF, I have hereunto set my hand and caused the seal of the State to be affixed this 14th day of March, in the year of Our Lord, one thousand nine hundred and fifty-five, and of Independence, the one hundred and seventy-ninth.

(signed) Dennis J. Roberts
Governor

THE FASCINATION OF TONY OAKES

Source: Hayward, [California] Journal, June
27, 1916; John Sandoval, "Portuguese take to
politics in grand fashion, " The Daily Bulletin
(Hayward, California), March 24, 1974.

A Portuguese-American with an Anglicized name, Anthony G. Oakes,
the "Tony" Oakes of California lore, was an innkeeper, war veteran, and
genial entertainer who in his day was widely known in the bay area and left
a mark on the Alameda county community of Hayward, where Oakes Boulevard perpetuates his memory.

He was born in Boston about the year 1828, the son of Portuguese parents who belonged to the pioneer whaling and codfishing colony of Massachusetts, and it was there, when the United States declared war on Mexico
in 1846, that he immediately volunteered to serve in a Massachusetts regiment.

He was with General Winfield Scott when the Americans captured Vera
Cruz. The hero of the War of 1812, taken by the boy's silvery tenor voice,
had him join his personal staff as mess attendant and entertainer.

It was while he was with the American occupying forces in Mexico City
that he heard about the fabulous land of Alta California. He had the foresight to provide himself with letters of introduction to General Mariano Vallejo, the cattle and land baron, and other Mexican officials in the San Francisco area. When he would get to California would depend on other circumstances.

While visiting his family in Massachusetts, having been mustered out
of the Army in 1847, word reached him of the California Gold Strike of
1848. This was the call to action. He booked passage to Panamá, crossed
the isthmus, found his way up the coast, and early in 1849 he was in San
Francisco.

General Vallejo was not keen on mining and suggested that the young
man use his talents as a cook. He got a job at Sonoma House, a hotel-sa-
loon on the Plaza in Sonoma -- it became the Blue Wing Hotel in 1853,
named after a bar in San Francisco -- where he got to know the businessmen of the place and entertained them in the evenings with his voice and
guitar.

In 1850 Oakes moved to the boomtown of San Francisco, where he went
into the restaurant business for himself, opening a lunch room on Kearney
Street. He was in San Francisco in 1851-1852 when the Vigilante Committee
of Elder Sam Brannan took it upon itself to clean out the lawbreakers from
Chiletown, under the lea of Telegraph Hill.

The Kearney Street lunch room was located near the pioneer theatre
district around the Plaza, and actors and singers from the Jenny Lind, the

Adelphi, the American, and the Metropolitan theatres, as well as from Tom Maguire's Opera House, dropped by Tony's place.

It became a hangout for important people of the times, men of the caliber of William Ralston (of Palace Hotel fame), James Lick, D.O. Mills, and "Lucky" Baldwin. And for politicians, too.

When he moved his business to Market Street, he took advantage of his reputation for seafood dishes and called the restaurant "The Terrapin Lunch."

In 1859, at Ralton's suggestion, he sold the Terrapin and bought the Crystal Springs Resort Hotel on the San Mateo-Spanish Town county road. Plagued by floods and bad loans, he gave up the Crystal Springs in 1863 and took over the San Mateo House on El Camino Real. The fire of November 7, 1863 wiped him out and forced him to move again. This time he moved to Redwood City, where he ran a hotel on the waterfront.

F.D. Atherton, who had bought the residual acreage of the Guillermo Castro Ranch at a sheriff's sale in 1865, convinced Oakes to move to Hayward with the promise to set him up in the hotel business. Within a short time, Oakes' Villa Hotel became known everywhere for its food, liquors, and entertainment. So popular did it become that in 1878 Oakes published his own songbook.

Because of the innkeeper's influence, western circuses began to winter in Hayward. "He built menageries and training sawdust rings behind his hotel and provided board and room to the acrobats, show freaks, animal trainers, clowns and equestrians...."

Oakes retired from innkeeping about 1890 and died in 1896. One of his sons from his marriage to a Petaluma girl in 1852, George Oakes, was the proprietor of the Hayward Journal, the community's leading newspaper. George, who was an active Republican, also served a four-year term as postmaster of Hayward.

Tony's line continues. In the Spring of 1974, George Oakes, Tony's great grandson, ran for the Hayward City Council.

THE PROTESTANT PORTUGUESE

Source: Walter deShara, "Group From Madeira Islands Settled in Jacksonville, Illinois, 102 Years Ago, " Standard-Times (New Bedford, Massachusetts), May 20, 1951; Leo Pap, "Portuguese pioneers and early immigrants in North America, " Actas, V Colóquio Internacional de Estudos Luso-Brasileiros, I (Coimbra, Portugal, 1965), 5-15.

The story is one of the 350 immigrants from the Island of Madeira, all converts to Protestantism, who reached Jacksonville, Illinois, in a roundabout way in 1849, and of the 300 other Madeirans who joined them in 1851. Not a sizable or overwhelming population, but a human collectivity of a special kind that served as an experiment in Americanization and produced surprising results.

In 1838, a young and personable Protestant medical missionary from Edinburgh, Scotland, Dr. Robert Reid Kalley, went to Madeira for reasons of health, liked the island so much that he decided to stay, and converted hundreds of islanders to his faith. Riots against the converts broke out in 1846, and in the same year Kalley took his followers to Trinidad, then under English control, to seek a more congenial religious environment on the sugar and cocoa plantations.

The conditions in Trinidad were unbearable and many of the refugees succumbed to the rigors of life on the Caribbean island. They then made arrangements with the American Hemp Company for settlement and employment in New Berlin, Illinois. The colonists arrived in New York on December 1, 1848, but the company failed to live up to its commitments and they were stranded there.

When word reached them of the plight of the Madeiran group, the principal Protestant churches of Jacksonville generously offered homes and employment to the exiles. The offer was gratefully accepted, and the Portuguese immigrants reached their destination in November, 1849. In 1853, the Madeiran settlers erected the first Portuguese Protestant church building, the forerunner of the Northminster Presbyterian Church.

The Portuguese established themselves on their small farms. They became the truck farmers, housemen, gardeners, and the like for the wealthier citizens of Jacksonville. One of their women became a trusted servant of the Abraham Lincoln family.

The first generation was obviously restricted by language and training to the lowest social rung. But there were exceptions. John C. Cherry, an illiterate Portuguese with an Anglicized name, became one of Jacksonville's leading businessmen, the owner of eighty-five large houses.

The second generation, having overcome the barriers, began to move upward. A number of them got jobs as railroad conductors and locomotive engineers. A man with a corrupted Portuguese name, Frank Meline, moved to Kansas City and then to Los Angeles. Here he earned a fortune in real estate and the laundry business. He laid out Beverly Hills and designed and built the Mary Pickford home. Another Portuguese, James P. DeMattoes (de Mattos) was the first of his race to graduate from college. He became a circuit judge and mayor of Bellingham, Washington.

Of the third generation Portuguese, five turned to medicine, some practiced law, and many entered the teaching profession. Mary Astor, the movie star, was the granddaughter of Frank Vasconcellos. Arthur Vasconcellos, known professionally as Art Concellos, was a trapeze artist with Ringling Brothers Barnum and Bailey Circus who later became the general manager of the Greatest Show on Earth. Mae deSouza, daughter of John deSouza, a lieutenant on the Chicago police force, was a famous opera singer at the turn of the century. Frank Martin (Martins) played first cornet with the John Philip Sousa band. And finally, Herbert R. Vasconcellos served Jacksonville, after 20 years as Morgan County Superintendent of Schools, in the highest elective office, that of mayor. It was a belated recognition and tribute to the progress of the Portuguese since the days of their humble beginnings.

The Portuguese also became part of the fraternal community, and they were especially active in Masonic organizations. They made their mark in organized labor as well and reached positions of responsibility in the movement. Cloyd deFreitas and Charles Souza served as president of the Jacksonville Trades and Labor Assembly.

As Walter deShara, himself a descendant of the Jacksonville pioneers, once wrote, "In any bargain, we are apt to think of someone profiting, someone losing. In this deal, however, without a shadow of a doubt, both Jacksonville and the Portuguese have profited handsomely. Not only have the Portuguese accommodated themselves to our way, but we are the better and stronger -- and even a little better looking for the bargain." There is no monument in stone to the Portuguese colonists of Jacksonville, but "Portuguese Hill" remains as a living witness to their presence.

The experience of the Jacksonville Portuguese is an example of the ease with which foreign elements were assimilated into the Anglo mainstream when Catholicism was not a factor. In other parts of the country, where the Portuguese remained faithful to their traditional religion, adjustment and acceptance by the wider community came more slowly. The price that the Jacksonville Portuguese paid for their integration was their disappearance as an ethnic group. So complete was their assimilation that they began to use corrupted family names and adopted the Protestant fashion of giving their children Old Testament names.

Was the price too high to pay?

SWEET DADDY GRACE

Source: New York Times, January 13, 1960;
The Washington Post, January 13, 1960; Joseph
R. Washington, Jr., Black Sects and Cults (New
York, 1972), pp. 10, 11, 12, 15-16, 77, 127, 149,
158-159.

Joseph R. Washington, Jr., is not sympathetic to the kind of religious
phenomenon that Sweet Daddy Grace represents. In the jargon of the social
sciences, he classifies Daddy Grace as a "cult personality," as indeed he
was, but Washington pays no attention to the fact that the flamboyant leader
established churches of his faith in some 110 cities of the United States,
with a membership in 1960 of about 3,000,000 people. One cannot hastily
dismiss the spiritual impact of the man in the face of these statistics.
    Charles Manuel Grace -- two of his names were anglicized -- the
Daddy Grace or Sweet Daddy Grace of his adoring followers, was born in
the Cape Verde Islands, apparently in 1882. He emigrated to the United
States and arrived in New Bedford, according to the most reliable sources,
in 1903.
    He was a cook on a Southern railway, and in the course of time came
under the influence of Holiness and Pentecostal teaching. In 1925 he was
called to "preach", assumed the name of "Grace", and proclaimed himself
a bishop. He exercised his episcopal prerogatives to the end.
    Bishop Grace's United House of Prayer for All People, Church On The
Rock Of The Apostolic Faith, with headquarters in Washington, D.C., began in 1926 with the founding of a congregation in Wareham, Massachusetts.
In the same year he founded another church, in Charlotte, North Carolina,
which had 13,000 members in 1960.
    Over the span of 30 years, he not only built houses of prayer through-
out the United States but he also acquired valuable properties in the major
cities. He maintained a mansion in Los Angeles, one in Montclair, New
Jersey, and another house on Logan Circle, Washington, D.C. He owned
a hotel in New York, a coffee fazenda in Brazil, a farm in Cuba. He loved
material things and he used them for spiritual purposes (along with erotic
dancing of a liturgical nature). When he died in Los Angeles on January 12,
1960, he had amassed a fortune of about $6,000,000. But he left it all to
his church.
    The body of the man who in life wore purple suits when it pleased his
fancy and allowed his manicured fingernails to grow long in the old Portuguese fashion -- a sign that he did no manual labor -- was claimed by two
sisters, Sylvia Gomes and Louise Grace. Sweet Dady Grace, who belonged
to the Cape Verdean community of New Bedford, Massachusetts, lies buried
among his own people.
    He is the only Portuguese who ever founded a church in the United States.

THE CARDINAL ARCHBISHOP OF BOSTON

Source: Who's Who in America, 37th edition,
1972-1973; Official Catholic Directory, 1974.

By virtue of his high post, His Eminence Humberto Sousa Medeiros,
Cardinal Archbishop of Boston, is far and above the most illustrious Portuguese-American of the United States.

Born in Arrifes, São Miguel, Azores, on October 6, 1915, he emigrated
to the United States in 1931 and began his career, like so many Portuguese
in similar circumstances, in the mills of the Fall River-New Bedford,
Massachusetts area. He became a naturalized American citizen in 1940.

Cardinal Medeiros has three degrees from The Catholic University of
America, the master of arts (1942), the licentiate in sacred theology (1946),
and the doctor of sacred theology (1959), and acquired at the University the
reputation of being a superb Latinist. In 1949-1950, he was in Rome, at
the North American College. Stonehill College, Massachusetts, conferred
upon him the degree of doctor of laws honoris causa in 1959.

Ordained to the priesthood in 1946, diocese of Fall River, his first and
very brief assignment was to the St. John of God parish, Somerset. In the
same year he was transferred to St. Michael's parish, Fall River. He was
moved in 1947 to another Fall River parish, that of Our Lady of Health. In
1948-1949 he directed the St. Vincent de Paul Camp for underprivileged
children. Following his appointment to Mount Carmel Church, New Bedford,
he left for Rome on a research project in 1949.

Upon his return to the United States in 1950, he served at Holy Name
Church, Fall River, and remained there until 1951. During 1951-1953, the
Cardinal was second assistant chancellor of his diocese, chaplain of the
Academy of the Sacred Hearts, and vicar for religious. From 1953-1966,
he served first as vice-chancellor and then as chancellor of the diocese of
Fall River. He was named a domestic prelate by the Holy Father in 1958.
He was pastor of St. Michael's parish, Fall River from 1960 to 1966. In
the latter year he was consecrated bishop of Brownsville, Texas. He became archbishop of Boston in 1970 and was elevated to the College of Cardinals on March 5, 1973.

Cardinal Medeiros, who is characterized by a deep spirituality and a
dedication to the pastoral ministry, is a member of several episcopal committees and of the Board of Trustees of The Catholic University of America,
his alma mater. Following his appointment to the College of Cardinals, His
Eminence visited the island of his birth, where he was triumphantly received.

A MAN OF VISION

Source: Carlos Almeida, "Antonio Fonte
pai ou padrinho?!...," União Portuguesa
do Estado da Califórnia Life (San Leandro,
California), LXIX, no. 3, July, 1970, 3,
5-6, 8, 14.

António Fonte, who founded on August 1, 1880 the União Portuguesa do
Estado da Califórnia (U.P.E.C.), one of the largest Portuguese fraternal
societies in the United States, was born in Pico, Azores, on February 25,
1826. He belonged to a generation of men of enormous stature but none exceeded him in experience and integrity.

He took to the sea at the age of 19 and plied between ports of England.
He later went to India, where he became involved in trading ventures. The
news of the Gold Rush must have reached him in the Orient and fired his
imagination. He sailed from Manila for California and arrived in San Francisco in 1851. He was not, however, attracted to mining, and stayed in the
bay area.

After working at minor jobs, he opened a boarding house in Oakland in
1854. He continued to direct the business almost uninterruptedly until 1861,
when he demolished the building on the site and erected another one, this
time a store, which he held on to for 40 years.

As his popularity grew, so also the demands upon his time. In a heavily
Republican constituency, Fontes was elected on the Democratic ticket as
treasurer of Alameda County. It was at about this time that he set up house-
keeping on his own, marrying Rosanna Lyons, a native of Ireland, from
whom he had five children.

On March 1, 1876, a group of concerned Portuguese met in San Leandro to discuss mutual aid. The recognized leader of the group was António
Fonte. What resulted was the establishment of the Portuguese Brotherhood
of the State of California (Irmandade Portuguesa do Estado da Califórnia),
the predecessor of Council No. 1 of the U.P.E.C., formally created on August 1, 1880.

When the Supreme Council of the U.P.E.C. was organized in 1887,
Pontes was elected its first president and served in this capacity until 1893
when he became Director of the society, a position of leadership he held until
his death on April 7, 1906. At the time of his death, at the age of eighty, the
U.P.E.C. had notably expanded its ranks and reached a total membership
of 7,000 California Portuguese.

He devoted the last years of his life to the society that he had founded,
but the U.P.E.C. was not his only love. He was the second president of the
Pacific Coast branch of the Catholic Mutual Benefit Association, and on another occasion was the Association's treasurer.

THE PORTUGUESE-AMERICAN BANK OF SAN FRANCISCO

Source: This text is based on The Hillhouse
Scrapbook (on the American Bank and its pre-
decessors), 11. 152-153, in the Wells Fargo
Bank History Room, 420 Montgomery Street,
San Francisco, California; Leroy Armstrong
and J. O. Denny, Financial California An Historical Review of the Beginnings and Progress
of Banking in the State (San Francisco: The Coast
Banker Publishing Company, 1961), p. 189; and
Ira B. Cross, Financing an Empire history of
banking in California (Chicago, San Francisco,
Los Angeles: The S.J. Clarke Publishing Co.,
1927), pp. 677, 681, 768.

The Portuguese-American bank of San Francisco was incorporated on
November 29, 1905, with a capital of $200,000 which was later raised to
$1,000,000. The original board of directors was composed of Manuel Teix-
eira Freitas, José Baptista, William H. Crocker, John Rafael, John Enos,
José S. Bello, J.M. Santana, B. Sherry, M.G. Lewis, and J.J. Enos. The
officers were Manuel Teixeira Freitas, president; Joaquim A. Silveira, re-
putedly the richest Portuguese in the United States, vice president; and
V. L. de Figueiredo, secretary.

William H. Crocker headed the subscription list of 153 stockholders.
Most of these were prominent in local Portuguese business circles. The
bank had its origin in the days just before the earthquake and fire of 1906.
Temporary quarters were opened in a store adjoining the Clay and Front
Streets bank site. Within three months it was located at the northeast cor-
ner of Sansome and Clay Streets.

The bank became about settled and prosperous when the fire of 1906
took everything with the exception of cash, securities and other valuables,
and the more important books of record. On the morning of April 18, these
were moved in haste to safe deposit vaults at the Crocker Bank where they
remained until the vaults cooled. Temporary quarters were then set up for
the bank at the Crocker Bank, corner of Clay and Laguna Streets.

The bank occupied a part of the Crocker Bank annex for a short time,
then moved to a temporary corrugated iron shack built at the northeast corner of Davis and Jackson Streets. The bank entered into an agreement with
the Marvin Estate to lease for ten years a three-story bank building to be
erected at the corner of Clay and Front Street. On completion, December
1, 1907, the bank moved to its new quarters. In time the premises were
acquired by the bank and here a bank functioned until February 27, 1937.

[According to Judge Carlos R. Freitas, of San Rafael, California, a son
of the bank's first president, the ground floor of the bank building was occu-

pied by the bank itself. The second floor was shared by Dr. J. de Faria, a Portuguese physician and surgeon, and by the Sherry-Freitas Company. This company, owned jointly by B. Sherry and Manuel Teixeira Freitas, sold dairy products in San Francisco under the trade name of "Sherreitas Butter." The top floor was occupied in its entirety by the Pacific Box Company. Before and after 1925, the second floor was occupied by the consulate general of Portugal. |

On September 11, 1912, the bank received authorization to open a branch at Newman; on August 8, 1914, in Oakland, at Eleventh and Franklin Streets. On May 3, 1921, the Portuguese-American Bank of San Francisco purchased the Los Banos Portuguese-American Bank, an independent bank organized on October 19, 1918. At the time of the purchase, the Los Banos bank had a capital of $50,000 and deposits of $112,000. The directors of the Los Banos bank, as of June 30, 1919, were B.J. Tognazzi, president; T.S. Garcia, Jr., vice-president; M.C. Gomes, J.C. Jacques, V. Rodrigues, W.E. Burch, and M.L. Rocha. R.P. Snyder was secretary. In 1920 William High succeeded as secretary, treasurer, and cashier, and there were also new directors, i.e. Joe Cardazi, Martin Errica, and J. Valladão.

At the close of business, December 31, 1923, the total resources of the Portuguese-American Bank of San Francisco amounted to $4,732,294.47. At this time Joaquim A. Silveira was president; A.F. Nunes, vice-president; H.B. Hunter, vice-president; V.L. de Figueiredo, cashier; and M.T. Bettencourt, Ed. Jerome, Joseph A. Enos, Frank D. Armstrong, M. Silva, Arthur J. Silva, and George M. Quintal, assistant cashiers. James B. Feehan was the attorney for the bank. The directors were Joaquim A. Silveira, A.F. Nunes, J.J. Nunes, H.B. Hunter, José Baptista, J.B. Mendonça, M.T. Azevedo, F.S. Soares, F.J. Cunha, and Joe Cardozo.

The bank merged with the Mercantile Trust Company of California on February 23, 1924, which in turn merged with the American Bank of San Francisco in 1927. In 1960 this bank was in turn acquired by the Wells Fargo Bank.

The Portuguese-American Bank of San Francisco was the most ambitious and successful banking operation ever attempted by the Portuguese people of the United States.

A PIONEER SCHOLAR

Source: The text, by the editor, is based substantially on Helen Coutinho, Pleasant recollections of Dr. Joaquim de Siqueira Coutinho
(New York: Saint Anthony Press, 1969).

Born in Lisbon on August 4, 1885, Dr. Joaquim de Siqueira Coutinho,
described by Monsignor Joseph Cacella as a man of genius, was educated in
the Portuguese capital and graduated with distinction from the School of
Economics and Political Science in 1904. Having also enrolled in the Lisbon
Institute of Technology, he received his diploma from that institution in 1907,
certified as a civil and electrical engineer. His advanced study took him to
England on a Portuguese government scholarship where he studied at the
University of London and at Oxford (1908-1910).

Upon his return to Lisbon in 1909, he joined the staff of the new Minister of the Interior, Colonel Dias Costa, as secretary for political and cultural affairs. In 1910 King Manuel II awarded him a knighthood in the Order
of Santiago. When the Portuguese republic was proclaimed on October 5,
1910, Dr. Coutinho, because he was a monarchist, left government service
to work for the Portuguese railroads (1910-1916).

In 1916, Dr. Coutinho came to America on a special mission of the Portuguese government, and here he was destined to stay. He became a good
friend of Dr. Domício da Gama, the Brazilian Ambassador, and this led to
his decision to make his home in Washington, D.C. From 1910-1920 he
was in charge of the Brazilian section of the Pan American Union and in this
capacity visited Brazil in 1918. From 1916-1925 he taught Portuguese at
The George Washington University. In 1920, at the invitation of the rector,
Bishop Thomas Shahan, he joined the faculty of The Catholic University of
America, where he assisted Dr. Manoel de Oliveira Lima, the distinguished
Brazilian diplomat and scholar, whose great library is described elsewhere
in these pages. In the same year he joined the faculty of the new School of
Foreign Service at Georgetown University, being the only surviving member
of the original faculty. In 1936 he taught geopolitics at Georgetown for the
first time in any American university. He had earlier retired from The
Catholic University of America, where his last assignment was that of director of the University Museum; in 1954, he brought his teaching career
to a close by becoming a professor emeritus of Georgetown University.

Dr. Coutinho has been the recipient of well-deserved accolades. His
first decoration, in the Portuguese Order of Santiago, a knighthood, was bestowed, as we have already seen, in 1910. In 1923 he was raised to the rank
of officer of the same Order. In 1963, the Portuguese government awarded
him a commandery in the Order of Prince Henry the Navigator. He has received medals from the Holy See, the Portuguese Red Cross, and from Ecua-

dor. He has the Pan American Medal. In 1960 Georgetown University remembered him with the Axacan Award.

His contributions to the spread of the language and literature of Portugal are legion, and his A Portuguese Grammar, published by D.C. Heath &
Co. in 1925 (with E.C. Hills of the University of California and J.D.M.
Ford of Harvard University) was used by numerous generations of students
in the United States as in other English-speaking countries.

In 1974, at the beginning of his 90th year, Dr. Coutinho still lives in
Washington, D.C., with his daughter and biographer, a medical doctor with
a degree from Marquette University. His son, John de Siqueira, having studied aeronautical engineering in Germany and in New York, is with the Grum-
man Aircraft Corporation on Long Island. Mrs. Coutinho, nee Louise Ger-
maine Hoare Vallet, of Lisbon, a talented concert pianist, died in Washington on October 2, 1939.

FRANCIS MILLET ROGERS

Source: The text is based on Who's Who in
America; Representative Men and Old Families of Southeastern Massachusetts, III (Chicago, 1912), 1652-1653); Francis M. Rogers
to Manoel da Silveira Cardozo, Cambridge,
December 9, 1974.

Francis Millet Rogers, the eminent Portuguese-American scholar, is
the descendant of Portuguese pioneers of Southeastern Massachusetts. His
paternal grandfater, Captain John Rogers, was born in Horta, Faial, Azores,
on February 2, 1837, ran away from home, and arrived at Stonington, Connecticut, on board the bark United States in May, 1853. As he entered the
country, an immigration officer took it upon himself to change the young
man's name from João da Rosa to John Rogers.

Rogers continued in the whaling business until 1892, and in the course
of his long career on the sea sailed as far as the Arctic fishing grounds via
the Bering Strait. In 1846, the year of the Irish Famine, he married an Irish
immigrant girl, Annie Conlin. Their son, Frank Leo, graduated from
Georgetown University, took a law degree at Boston University, and married
Laura, daughter of the Portuguese-American Sylvia family of New Bedford.
He is the father of Francis Millet Rogers, who first saw the light of day in
New Bedford on November 26, 1914.

The third-generation Francis, whose Portuguese studies have characterized his professional life, became attracted to the language of his Portuguese forbears during his freshman year at Cornell University, an interest
that his Irish grandmother, who lived with the Rogers family, enormously
fostered. The attraction continued all during his university training and led
to a Ph.D. dissertation in 1940 at Harvard University. With American par-
ticipation in the Second World War, he saw active duty with the Marine
Corps as a lieutenant colonel. Promoted to colonel, he resigned his commission in 1968.

His career at Harvard began when he joined the faculty in 1946 and there
he has remained ever since. He became a full professor in 1952. He has
served on various occasions as chairman of the Department of Romance
Languages and Literatures, and from 1949 to 1955 as dean of the Graduate
School of Arts and Sciences. He has been involved with the International Association of Universities and the Institute of International Education. He was
president of the First International Colloquium on Luso-Brazilian Studies,
Washington, D.C., 1950, and had a hand in organizing the 1966 Colloquium.
He belongs to numerous academic societies, including Phi Beta Kappa and
the Society for the History of Discoveries. He was president of the latter
from 1968 to 1969. He is an honorary professor of the University of San
Marcos, Lima, Peru (1961), a chevalier of the Legion of Honor (France),

and has honorary doctorates from eight American and one Brazilian institutions of higher learning.

He has contributed articles on Portuguese linguistics, literature, and
maritime history to learned journals and he is the author of seven book,
i.e. Higher Education in the United States: A Summary View (1952; 3d ed.
1960), The Obedience of a King of Portugal (1958), The Travels of the In-
fante Dom Pedro of Portugal (1961); The Quest for Eastern Christians (1962);
Europe informed: An Exhibition of Early Books Which Acquainted Europe
with the East (1966); Precision Astrolabe: Portuguese Navigators and Trans-
oceanic Aviation (1971), and Americans of Portuguese Descent: A Lesson
in Differentiation (1974).

Professor Rogers also keeps the home fires burning. He was a trustee
of the Old Dartmouth Historical Society and of the Whaling Museum, New
Bedford, Massachusetts (1970-1973). Since 1968, he has been a trustee of
St. John's Seminary, Boston.

Francis Millet Rogers is the outstanding Portuguese scholar of his generation and amply deserves the acclaim that he has received. João da Rosa's
grandson (with a powerful assist from his Irish grandmother) is proof
enough of the perennial vitality of the stock.

JORGE DE SENA

Source: A text based on the curriculum vitae
supplied by the biographee, December 27, 1974.

Jorge de Sena is far from being the typical Portuguese immigrant. Had
it not been for the political situation in Portgual, which was not to his liking,
he would not have sought a more congenial life in Brazil, and if the Brazlian
revolution of 1964 had not taken place, inevitably creating problems for the
Portuguese exile, it is not likely that he would have come to the United States.
A victim of the condition of men of independent thought in our time, Jorge de
Sena, from his refuge in Santa Barbara by the sea, surrounded by an adoring
wife and nine children, maintains intimate literary and political ties with
the Portuguese homeland, and, unlike his fellow immigrants who have also
taken to the pen, is a literary figure of distinguished prominence in the country of his origin.

Born in Lisbon in 1919, he was trained in civil engineering at the University of Oporto. For fifteen years he practiced his profession and concur-
rently developed his talents as a man of letters and public speaker. In 1959,
following the unsuccessful presidential campaign of General Humberto Del-
gado, Jorge de Sena moved to Brazil, where he became a university professor and earned a doctorate in Portuguese literature. In 1965 he moved again,
this time to Madison, to teach Portuguese at the University of Wisconsin.
Later he accepted an appointment at the University of California, Santa Barbara, where he teaches Portuguese and Brazilian literature and serves as
chairman of the Comparative Literature Program.

He made his debut in Portuguese letters in 1938. His first book of
poems, Perseguição, was published in 1942, the first work of surrealistic
inspiration to appear in Portugal. Other works from his pen followed, in an
almost unending succession. Not content with these achievements, he has
published translations of poetry from a variety of ancient and modern literatures. His excursion into drama began with a four-act tragedy in verse,
O indesejado (António Rei) (1951), considered one of the most significant
works of the Portuguese theatre. Since then, he has produced short pieces
for the stage as well. In still another field of creativity, he is the author of
highly experimental short stories. And finally, as a scholar, he has written
numerous studies and monographs in literary history and criticism. His
work on Luís de Camões, which he presented at the Portuguese Cultural Institute of Paris, was in many ways the highlight of the 1972 anniversary of
the fourth centennial of the publication of The Lusiads.

Jorge de Sena is not only widely known among the Portuguese of Califor-
nia--his public lectures attract a devoted following--and of Portugal, where
his books are in every bookstore, but also abroad, wherever his poetry has
been published in English, French, German, Spanish, Italian, Rumanian, Lithu-
anian, and Croatian translations (not to speak of some of his short stories
which have appeared in German and Dutch translations).

A DISTINGUISHED LIBRARY

Source: A text based on Manoel Cardozo's "In-
troduction, " Catalog of the Oliveira Lima Library
The Catholic University of America Washington,
D.C., I (Boston: G. K. Hall & Co., 1970), p. iii

The Oliveira Lima Library, founded in 1916 and opened to the public
in 1924, is a widely known repository of bibliographical and other items
that illustrate for the most part the history and culture of the Portuguese-
speaking poeples. It is the oldest and most distinguished library of its kind
in the United States, and it ranks high among specialized Luso-Brazilian libraries anywhere. Located in its own quarters in the John K. Mullen of
Denver Memorial Library on the campus of The Catholic University of
America, Washington, D.C., the Oliveira Lima Library, in its organization and premises, preserves much of the original atmosphere and flavor
of Brazil's belle époque.
   The founder of the Library, Manoel de Oliveira Lima (1867-1928), the
Brazilian son of a Portuguese father, was an historian of international reputation, a diplomat and journalist who collected printed books, manuscripts,
and objects of art. During his lifetime he made use of them assiduously in
his research and writing. Since his death, the resources of the Library,
systematically improved and enlarged, while continuing to serve newer generations of readers, remain as a monument to his foresight and the permanent values of the Luso-Brazilian world.
   The impression of a museum created by family portraits and memora-
bilia, the Frans Post landscape and mahogany cabinets filled with rare books,
is somewhat deceptive because visitors to the public rooms hardly suspect
that behind locked doors there is a stack area with almost 51,000 volumes,
some of them so unique that no other copies exist in the United States. Nor
do friends of the Library who have not seen it in many years realize that
the primitive collection of 16,000 volumes, which dates from 1916, has in
the intervening decades grown to its present substantial size.   ·
   The Library's holdings are of interest primarily for scholars in Portuguese and Brazilian history and literature and in the history and ethnography
of the present and former Portuguese territories or spehres of influence
overseas. The geographical areas covered in some way by the Library are
therefore enormous and range from Europe to the New World and beyond
to the Far East, India, and Africa. It is true that the Library has limited
collections on countries that have had historical connections with Brazil
and Portugal or with the subject of the Founder's personal interest, but
even when we bear this in mind the Library is characteristically Luso-Bra-
zialian.
   [The Founder of the Library, a native of Pernambuco, Brazil, was an
historian of international reputation, a diplomat, and a journalist who col-

lected books, manuscripts, and objects of art. Educated in Portugal, he entered the diplomatic service of Brazil in 1890, serving successively in Lisbon, Berlin, Washington, London, Tokyo, Caracas, and Brussels-Stockholm. He is the author of numerous historical works, especially remembered for his classic studies on the monarchy in Brazil. Among his many other actvities, he lectured at the Sorbonne (1911), at Stanford University (1912), served as visiting professor at Harvard University (1915), and inaugurated the chair of Brazilian studies at the University of Lisbon (1923). He was a founding member of the Brazilian Academy of Letters (the first to hold the Varnhagen chair), a member of the Brazilian Historical and Geographical Institute, and a corresponding member of the Lisbon Academy of Sciences. As a journalist, a career which he began early in life, he contributed to newspapers and periodicals in Portugal, France, Brazil, and Argentina. During the last years of his life, he was an associate professor of international law at The Catholic University of America. He died in Washington, D.C.]

THE UKULELE IS PORTUGUESE

Source: A text based on Anthony J. Drexel
Biddle, The Madeira islands, I (Philadelphia,
1900), 263; Samuel H. Elbert and Edgar C.
Knowlton, Jr., "Ukulele," American Speech,
XXXII, no. 4 (December 1957), 307-310.

The ukulele, the Hawaiian national instrument, is of Madeiran origin.
Anthony J. Drexel Biddle described the Portuguese prototype of the ukulele
in 1900. The Madeirans, he said, "have an instrument peculiar to their use
and called the machete, which when well played produces very sweet strains;
in appearnce it resembles closely a small guitar, though it has but four
strings, all of catgut. The upper two are tuned in thirds, and the lower two
in fourths. While the native melodies consist in a succession of simple
chords, the most difficult and classical music can be agreeably rendered
upon it."

Two knowledgeable Americans, Samuel H. Elbert and Edgar C. Knowlton, Jr., are of the opinion that the Hawaiian ukulele is an adaptation of an
instrument called braga, machete de braga, or braguinha in Portuguese.
(In the Azores, Brazil, and other parts of the Portuguese-speaking world, it
is also known as cavaquinho.)

Among the immigrants from Madeira who got to Hawaii in 1879 were
three instrument makers by the names of Augusto Dias, Manuel Nunes, and
Z. Santos. It is to them that we owe the ukulele, an imported idea that caused
the Hawaiians to lose interest in their native instruments and adopt as their
own the immigrant version of the cavaquinho of Madeira.

The name "ukulele" was given to the new instrument by Portuguese cane
cutters in Hawaii, and how this came about is explained by Elbert and Knowlton. "The machete was heard one day by the vice-chamberlain of King Kalakaua's court, who was so delighted that he asked to be taught to play it.
Soon thereafter he began to perform at the king's court. This vice-chamberlain was a British army officer named Edward Purvis, but the Hawaiians,
fond of nicknames, called him ukulele because his lively playing and antics
and his small build suggested a leaping flea. The new instrument became
a great success, and even the king learned to play. Augusto Dias made instruments commercially, and someone started calling them ukulele, the
nickname of Edward Purvis. These instruments were somewhat smaller
than those from the island of Madeira." Another source credits Manuel
Nunes with having introduced the ukulele to the Hawaiian Islands in 1879;
because of his instrument he became a great favorite of King Kalakaua, who
encouraged him to manufacture it.

There is no question about the Portuguese origin of the favorite instrument of the islands.

PORTUGUESE AND THE UNIVERSITY OF HAWAII
Concurrent Resolution of the Hawaiian Legislature

Source: Journal of the House of Representatives
of the Twentieth Legislature of the Territory of
Hawaii regular session, 1939 (Honolulu, 1939),
p. 341.

WHEREAS, the University of Hawaii already offers courses in the Japanese, Chinese, German, French and Spanish languages; and

WHEREAS, there are many persons of Portuguese extraction in the
Territory of Hawaii, and more and more of their children are attending the
University of Hawaii; and

WHEREAS, Portuguese is spoken over a larger area and among more
people than is Spanish; and

WHEREAS, with increased friendly relations between the United States
and the Latin American countries, particularly Brazil, the ability to read
and speak the Portuguese language will be of great benefit; now, therefore,
be it

RESOLVED by the House of Representatives of the Territory of Hawaii,
the Senate concurring, that the proper authorities be, and they hereby are
requested to provide in the curriculum of the University of Hawaii, beginning
with its next semester, a full credit course in the Portuguese language; and
be it further

RESOLVED that copies of this Concurrent Resolution be transmitted to
the Board of Regents of the University of Hawaii and to the President of the
University of Hawaii.

Offered by:

M.G. PASCHOAL
Representative, 3rd District

Seconded by

Mr. Costa.

JOHN PHILIP SOUSA

Source: A text based on Ann M. Lingg, John
Philip Sousa (1954); Herbert Weinstock, "John
Philip Sousa, " The Encyclopedia Americana XXV
(1970), 284-285; John Philip Sousa, Marching
Along (1925); and Grande Enciclopedia Portuguesa
e Brasileira (Lisbon), XXIX, 805; with additions
and revisions by Thomas Adams Sousa, Palo Alto,
California, John Philip Sousa's grandson, December 21, 1974.

John Philip Sousa belongs to the gallery of Americans of Portuguese descent because his father, João António de Sousa, an accomplished musician
in his own right who played with the United States Marine Band for twenty-
five years, was Portuguese. The elder Sousa was actually born in Spain, but
his Spanish birth was accidental. If his parents had not fled across the bor-
der, possibliy because of political upheavals at home, João António would
hve been born in Portugal.

João António, who changed his name to John Antonio Sousa and, when he
was naturalized, simply to Antonio Sousa, was not the run-of-the-mill immigrant. He may have even been related to the illustrious house that produced
Friar Luís de Sousa (1555-1632). The Lord Mayor of Liverpool suggested
as much on February 28, 1903, at the luncheon given in honor of John Philip,
when he presented the eminent musician with a copy of the 1795 London edition of James Murphy's treatise on the abbey church of Batalha (where Prince
Henry the Navigator lies buried). Appended to the Murphy text is Friar
Luís's description of the same great building.

The founder of the world's most famous concert band was born in Washington, D. C., on November 6, 1854, and studied the violin and composition in
his native city. When he wanted to run away with a circus at the age of thirteen, his father enlisted him in the Marines as a boy musician. At sixteen
he was already conducting theater orchestras. In 1876-1877, when J. Offen-
bach visited the United States, young Sousa played under his baton.

He directed the United States Marine Band from 1880 to 1892, resigning
the post to start his own band, the celebrated Sousa Band, which played its
first public concert in Plainfield, New Jersey, on September 26, 1892, and
which traveled altogether for some forty years. In 1900, 1901, 1903, and 1905,
he took the band to Europe. In 1910-1911, he went on a tour around the
world, delighting audiences everywhere with his music. When the First
World War broke out, John Philip Sousa, then sixty-two, disbanded his band
and joined the Navy as a lieutenant commander. He was sent to the Great
Lakes to train Navy bands. After the war, he reactivated his own band.

He became especially known for his marches -- "Stars and Stripes For-
ever, " "Semper Fidelis, " "The Washington Post March, " "Hands Across

the Sea"-- but he also composed operettas (El Capitan, The Charlatan, The Bride Elected, The Queen of Hearts, Mystical Miss) and several suites for piano ("The Chariot Race, " "The Last Days of Pompeii"). He was the author of 100 marches and 30 songs, symphonic poems, waltzes, etc. He wrote teaching manuals for the piano and drums. In 1890 he brought out a collection of National, Patriotic and Typical Airs of All Countries. To the novel, he contributed The Fifth String, Pipetown, Sandy, Through the Years, and Transit of Venus. In 1925 he published his auto-biography, Marching Along. He also designed a musical instrument known as the Sousaphone, in effect a modified Helicon tuba that diffuses the sound over the musicians instead of shooting it straight ahead.

This extraordinary man, the March King par excellence, whose music is part of the owrld's repertoire, and whose passage through life continues to be studied and acclaimed, died of a heart attack in Reading, Pennsylvania, on March 10, 1932, where he had gone as a guest conductor, at the end of a banquet in his honor. This may not have been the most dignified way to go, but it was typical of him to have died with his boots on.

There are memorials to him that keep before the public the singular achievements of a man whose musical genius symbolized an age. The huge collection of the Sousa Band's arrangements that were taken on tour are in a special Sousa Room in the music building at the University of Illinois. In 1974 he was elected to New York University's Hall of Fame for Great Ameri-cans, and eventually his bust will be seen by visitors in a place of honor. Washington, D.C., his home town, has especially taken him to heart. The John Philip Sousa Bridge over the Anacostia River, on Pennsylvania Avenue and Barney Circle, was dedicated in 1941; the John Philip Sousa Junior High School, in southeast Washington, in 1951. The stage in the Concert Hall of the John F. Kennedy Center for the Performing Arts is now officially known as the Sousa Stage. Practically all of the holographs of his music are in the Music Division of the Library of Congress. (Some of it has never been pub-lished.) At the Washington Navy Yard, the Marine Corps will soon open its Bands Americana Museum. Featuring the history of American bands since the American Revolutution, it will be built around the Sousa Band. Finally, a portrait of John Philip Sousa, the gift of the family, hangs in the National Portrait Gallery. He belongs there, alongside other Americans who have brought credit to their country.

JOHN DOS PASSOS (1896-1970)

Source: This text is based largely on the long
personal friendchip between the editor of this
volume and John Dos Passos, whose widow
helped in supplying the personal data. A piece
by William F. Buckley, Jr., which appeared
in the Evening Star is listed in its original form.

John Dos Passos died in Baltimore on September 28, 1970. He was the
most distinguished survivor of a distinguished literary generation, the only
American author of Portuguese descent with an international reputation.

Born in Chicago on January 14, 1896, he was the son of John R. Dos Passos, a noted corporation lawyer, and grandson of Manoel dos Passos, a native of Ponta do Sol, Madeira, who emigrated to the United States in or
about 1830. He graduated from Harvard University with a bachelor of arts
degree in 1916.

The career of John Dos Passos is so well known, so much a part of the
American literary scene, that a retelling of its highlights would be a redun-
dancy. He lived the full life of a practicing artist and of a country gentleman on a vast landed property in Westmoreland, Virginia, on the banks of
the Potomac River, which his provident father had acquired.

The public was not aware of the Portuguese side of John Dos Passos'
personality, yet he retained until the end of his life an attachment to the
country that gave him his name. He read Portuguese with facility and spoke
it. A few years before his death, he returned with his family to the island
of Madeira, the land of his paternal grandfather, where he was given a '
hero's welcome. Two books in particular give evidence of the strength of
his ancestral ties, Brazil on the move (1963) and The Portugal story (1969).

William F. Buckley, Jr., was among the mourners at the funeral of
John Dos Passos in Towson, Maryland. On October 7, 1970 The Evening
Star of Washington, D. C., published Buckley's eulogy of his friend.

"I have come back from the funeral of John Dos Passos. It was in a way
typical of him to die a few minutes after Nasser, who of course swamped
the obituary headlines, so much so that Dos Passos' own young stepson,
away at law school, who reads the papers lackadaisically and listens not at
all to the radio or TV, was not aware of the death until a few hours before
the funeral, to which he hastened, registering the grief felt universally by
everyone who had known Dos Passos, let alone been brought up by him.

"There was no way to keep his death off the front page -- geniuses have
a preemptive right to die on the front page -- but the reader felt that the
editorial handling was somehow harassed. Nasser had died, and the chan-
celleries of the world were in turmoil, and the death of mere literary giants
doesn't substantially occupy the front page (nor should it: Front pages are

correctly devoted to news of immediate and transitory significance. Never mind that few people can now remeber who reigned over England and Spain during the week that Shakespeare and Cervantes died.)

"On the other hand it is worth noting that Dos Passos did not suffer the pains that torture those artists who cry over the neglect of them by their contemporaries. The only reason he did not treat the literary press with the total aloofness of, say, an Edmund Wilson, or a Charles Lindbergh, is that he was too good natured.

"Did this mean that he had no self-esteem? No, that would be inaccurate. It means that he was a genuine artist, who did the very best he could every time he sat down to write a novel, or a book of history; but that since he had absolutely nothing to contribute to the improvement of a book after it was published, what was the point in reading reviews of his books? Or -- for heaven's sakes -- reviews of himself, as author of said books?

"We are talking about someone who stupefied the literary generation of the Twenties. Critics as disparate as Jean Paul Sartre and Whittaker Chambers were to remark matter-of-factly that he was the greatest novelist in America. The formal tributes did not, all of them, come in.

"It was an open secret that he was scorned by the Nobel Prize committee because of his political sympathies. He began his career as an ardent sympathizer of left-wing political movements. After the Spanish Civil War, he identified the Communists as the great evildoers of his time, an insight that caused him to do that which pained him most, namely to break a friendship: In this case, with Ernest Hemingway. But he pursued his conviction, that man was best off untrammeled by political authority, and of course when he died, the obituarists merely repeated what had been said about him so often before, namely that his literary work was at the service of political reactionaries.

"Translation: JDP was a political conservative, and the rules of the game being that no one can simultaneously be a literary genius and a political conservative, you must draw your own conclusions about Dos Passos. In the event that you are slow at doing that kind of thing, here is the key: JDP was a genius during his left-wing period. After that, he was pedestrian, a time-server. Never mind the two dozen books he wrote, the extraordinary histories of Jefferson, of Brazil, of Portugal; the novel 'Mid-Century.' Forget them, if you can.

"The answer is that no one can forget Dos Passos, and the working press somehow, sensed it. The reporters and the television people were at his funeral. I was accosted by one, who asked me to assess the literary work of JDP.

"I was at that moment in the company of John Chamberlain, whom William Lyon Phelps once called the principal literary critic of his generation, and to open my voice on Dos Passos in Chamberlain's presence would have been doubly to profane the situation inasmuch as what I wanted to say was simply that I would have been present, here at the Episcopal Church of Towson, Md., as sorrowfully if JDP had never written a word, because I knew him primarily as a friend but if literary taxonomy was what the press wanted, why didn't they ask Chamberlain?

"The widow, firm, tall, beautiful, moved serenely through the vague confusion, the result of an uneasy apprehension that the death of this modest man who came closest to explaining America to the world, might just turn out to be a historical event the neglect of which would above all proclaim the philistinism of the country he loved so very much more than his literary detractors love it.

"It was all so very hard to sort out, because the historical meaning of the occasion was clearly secondary to all who were there except the press. I traveled to Baltimore with an extraordinarily self-disciplined attorney (it was his 70th birthday) who had known JDP for fifty years, and on three occasions, my traveling companion had to turn away from a conversation, overcome by tears at the awful prospect of facing life without the freindship of John Dos Passos. If C.D. Batchelor were active, he'd have done a drawing of the Statue of Liberty weeping over this loss: This irreparable loss."

THE GREAT GILDERSLEEVE

Source: This text is based on a news release
supplied by the J.A. Freitas Library, San
Leandro, California.

Harold Peary was born Harrold José Pereira da Silva in San Leandro,
California, on July 25, 1908. What happened to his name is what has often
happened to other Portuguese names: he felt the social pressures of the
society in which he lived and changed it to Harold Perry. Later, a reporter
for the Oakland Tribune spelled young Hal's name as though he were related
to Robert E. Peary, the reputed discoverer of the North Pole. He wasn't
related at all, but the name stuck.

He was born on Dabney Street, named after his maternal great-grand-
father, João Guilherme Dabney, who emigrated from the Azores to Northern California via New Bedford, Massachusetts, in the early 1860s, and
educated in parochial schools in California, by private tutors, and at St.
Joseph's College, Yokohama, Japan. He took voice and drama lessons, and
then made his debut as a legitimate actor in 1925 at the Maud Fulton Playhouse in Oakland. He spent the next five years in comic opera, musical
comedy, and dramatic stock companies on the West Coast, the Orient, and
Australia.

Instead of finishing his college education, Peary was persuaded in January, 1930, to sign a six-month contract with the Western Division of the National Broadcasting Company in San Francisco. In 1935 he moved to Chicago,
where he played in radio "soap operas" and "kid shows." He signed an ex-
clusive arrangement with NBC in Chicago and was soon heard on such shows
as "Flying Time," "Girl Alone," Mary Marlin," "Grand Hotel" and "First
Nighter," with Don Ameche; "Light's Out" for Arch Oboler. On the Tom
Mix series, Peary played as many as eight character roles and sang the
theme song with a young actor, singer, and guitar player by the name of
George Gobel.

He played his first part on the "Fibber McGee and Molly" show in 1937.
A few weeks later the part of Throckmorton P. Gildersleeve was created
for him on the same show.

When the sponsors of "Fibber" moved the show to the Hollywood studios
of NBC in 1939, Peary went back to his native state, but it meant giving up
nine other radio shows in Chicago. Once in the movie capital, the talented
Peary made two films at RKO, one with "Fibber and Molly" and one with
Edgar Bergen and "Charley McCarthy" in 1940. He made a third movie with
Bob Burns at Paramount.

In 1941 Peary began his own radio series, "The Great Gildersleeve,"
broadcast over NBC in Hollywood. He was the first stooge to climb to radio
stardom.

He receive first-feature billing in "Seven Days' Leave," a motion picture starring Lucille Ball and Victor Mature. RKO signed Peary to star in a "Gildersleeve" series and five films were produced between 1942 and 1944. At the same time he recorded five albums for Capitol Records, "Gildersleeve's Stories for Children," which were widely sold. His fame as "Gildersleeve" was now assured.

In 1951, after ten successful years in radio, "The Great Gildersleeve" turned his back on NBC and moved to CBS for "The Hal Peary Show." It lasted a year, after which he went on a personal appearance tour of hotels and nightclubs to pave the way for a TV series that he wanted to do.

He starred on the Schlitz Playhouse with a half-hour TV show, "Papa goes to the ball," a comedy about a Portuguese-American family in the Monterey bay area of California. It was intended to arouse interest in a series that he had planned, "Call me papa," featuring the role of an Azorean-born fisherman, a widower with two teenage children, but the series didn't sell. Peary could only be "Gildersleeve" to the American public.

In the fall of 1954, he did a daily "disc jockey" stint over radio station WMGM, New York. Nine months later he was in Hollywood, doing the same thing for KABC, the ABC network station. In 1956 he starred as master of ceremonies on "Waltz Varieties," a live TV show in KCOP.

In the following year Peary left broadcasting to play in June Havoc's Desilu TV series, "Willy." In 1958, he played Herb Woodley in the "Blondie" series. He had featured roles in two Hollywood motion pictures of 1957-1958, that of a Portuguese tuna boat skipper in "Port of Hell" and of a Mexican racketeer in "Wetbacks." He was a guest on the Milton Berle, Bob Cummings, Betty Hutton, and Ray Bolger shows. In 1959, NBC contracted Peary to play his old "Gildersleeve" role in the TV version of "Fibber McGeee and Molly." It lasted 26 weeks and had several reruns.

He appeared in Walt Disney movies, on the Dick Van Dyke show, the Lucy Show, the Bill Bailey Show, the Dupont Show of the Month. He was on personal tours in New England. His three-day appearance in New Bedford in July, 1964, drew 100,000 people for the Portuguese-American festival of the Blessed Sacrament. During that summer he appeared in summer stock in New Jersey and Massachusetts.

Since then, he has continued his professional interests but from his home base in Manhattan Beach, California, his permanent address since 1957, where he supervises his rental properties in Manhattan Beach and San Diego county.

During his "Gildersleeve" days, he was named honorary water commissioner by four states and thirteen cities, including New York, Los Angeles, Oakland, Portland, and Reno. He is honorary mayor of San Leandro and Manhattan Beach and honorary chief of police of Redondo Beach.

Despite the establishment quality of his name, Harold Peary is proud of his Portuguese ancestry and speaks the language of his progenitors. His fellow Portuguese-Americans are proud of him too. No more distinguished radio personality has ever emerged from the Portuguese-American community of the United States.

CHAMPAGNE TONY

Source: This text is based in part on the dedication program of the Tony Lema Clubhouse at
San Leandro, California, and also on a letter from
Mrs. Clotilde Lema to Manoel da Silveira Cardozo, January 20, 1975.

How many golfers still remember Tony Lema, born on February 25,
1934, the "Champagne Tony" of golf fame, who was tragically killed at the
height of his career in an airplane crash on July 24, 1966? Those who follow
the game with professional interest and are familiar with its lore will not
easily forget the debonnair Californian of Portuguese descent -- his father's
parents were natives of Santa Maria, Azores, who emigrated to Bermuda
before moving to California at the time of the First World War -- the young
man who brought unrehearsed class to the sport. He was one of the first
Big Timers.

On May 31, 1974, Tony Lema was remembered by the San Leandro
(California) Marina Golf Course, supported by the San Leandro Golf Club
and the Marina Women's Golf Club, with the dedication of its new clubhouse
and the unveiling of the appropriate plaque.

The Dedication Program had this to say about Tony Lema:

"The dedication of the Tony Lema Clubhouse is a tribute to an outstanding golfer. He grew up in San Leandro, attending school at St. Joseph's,
Alameda, and St. Bernard's and St. Elizabeth's in Oakland. Beginning his
career as a caddy at the age of twelve, and later becoming a professional
golfer, Tony won his first prestigious tournament in 1957, the Imperial
Valley Open. He joined the P.G.A. Tour full-time in 1958.

"Throughout his career, ending tragically in 1966, Tony regarded San
Leandro as his real home. The following are some of his accomplishments
and professional tournament wins:

"1957.   Imperial Valley open, Idaho Open, and Montana Open.
"1962.   Orange County Open (Became known as Champagne Tony).
"1963.   Ryder Cup team member; Memphis Open.
"1964.   Bing Crosby Invitational, Thunderbird Open, Buick Open,
         Cleveland Open, and British Open.
"1965.   World Series of Golf, Carling World Open, and Buick Open.
"1966.   Oklahoma Open.

"At the time of his death he had climbed to tenth place on the All-time
P.G.A. money list. He was also the third man in the history of golf, behind
Arnold Palmer and Jack Nicklaus, to win over $100,000 in a single season.
It is in membery of Tony Lema that this Golf Clubhouse is dedicated on
May 31st, 1974."

JOHN G. MATTOS, JR.

Source: This text is based on Carlos Almeida,
"Men in our Country, " U.P.E.C. Life (San Leandro, California), LXX, No. 2 (April, 1971), 4.

In 1898, the Washington Press of Washington Township, Alameda County,
California, wrote with extraordinary obliquity: "Self-made men are a scar-
city in this township, yet we have several who are making their mark in the
world. " One of them was a Portuguese immigrant by the name of John G.
Mattos, Jr., born João Garcia Mattos, Jr., on August 1, 1864 in Angústias,
Horta, Faial, Azores, who went to California with his parents in 1870.

Settling in Centerville, Mattos became a naturalized American citizen
on July 31, 1886 and an active member of the Republican Party. He was
elected Road Overseer of the Centerville district in 1888, his first public
office, and reelected in 1890. From 1801 to 1895 he served as a Deputy
County Assessor for Washington Township. He was elected to his first term
on the Centerville School Board in 1893 and continued as a member for
thirty-five years. In August, 1897, he was admitted to the California Bar.
In the course of his legal career, he maintained offices in Centerville and
in San Francisco.

In 1900 Mattos was elected to the State Assembly for the forty-sixth
district, and reelected in 1902. He served one term in the State Senate,
1904-1908. In 1907 President Theodore Roosevelt named him Appraiser of
Merchandise at the Port of San Francisco, a position he held until 1914.
From 1918 to 1926, he served, by appointment of Governor Stephens, as a
member of the Board of Prison Directors.

When the Bank of Centerville was organized, Mattos was chosen as the
first president and served in this capacity until 1919. In this year the bank
was sold to the Bank of Italy of San Francisco. He later was a vice-president and a director of the Bank of Italy (whose name was later changed to
Bank of America).

His roster of public service would not be complete if we did not point
out that he was Justice of the Peace of Washington Township for eight years.

Mattos was active in Portuguese affairs too. He joined Council No. 5,
Centerville, of the União Portuguesa do Estado da Califórnia (U.P.E.C.) on
August 12, 1888. He was supreme president of the parent organization in
1894 and 1895 and supreme treasurer from 1898 through 1929.

This civic-minded Portuguese-American died on June 26, 1933. A public
school in the Fremont district of Centerville is named after him, a "testi-
monial to his long services to education and his community. "

THE FREITAS FAMILY: FATHER AND SON

Source: This text is based on information
from The Terra Linda News (California),
May 15, 1974; Independent-Journal (San Ra-
fael, California), May 25, 1924; Carlos R.
Freitas to Manoel da Silveira Cardozo, San
Rafael, September 25, 1974.

"Rich Destiny for Penniless Portuguese Immigrant" / "Manuel T. Freitas climbs from dishwasher to bank president" / "San Rafael's dairying
magnate had all of Terra Linda for his ranch and home."

In 1974 the city of San Rafael, California, celebrated its 100th birthday,
and The Terra Linda News, in its centennial edition of May 15, 1974, head-
lined the lead story in this extravagant way. The most remarkable thing
about the editor's choice of words is that they are literally true.

Born on São Jorge, Azores, Manuel Teixeira Freitas was only seventeen,
illiterate and penniless but stouthearted, when he arrived in San Francisco.
The year was 1870. He got a job in the restaurant kitchen of the old Portuguese Hotel, on Clay Street near the Embarcadero, and soon began to shape
his spectacular career. Within a short time, the employee was the owner
of the restaurant, and then of the hotel.

In the 1880s, having become a commission merchant, he moved to San
Rafael, where he began to amass the fortune that would distinguish him. In
1896, when he married seventeen-year-old Maria Bettencourt, the daughter
of a Portuguese dairy rancher from nearby Corte Madera and an early graduate of Dominican Convent, he was already, at the age of forty-three, a rich
man.

In 1905 the Portuguese-American Bank of San Francisco was organized.
He was the first president and a member of the board of directors. In 1906
he opened the Azores Mercantile Company, a retail clothing store at 66 Jackson Street, San Francisco. In 1911, with A.W. Foster, he founded the Bank
of San Rafael, now the Crocker Citizens National Bank. In 1915, the year of
the Panama Pacific International Exposition, he was the acting consul of Portugal in San Francisco.

In the course of his long and active career, this pioneer Portuguese-
American owned a half interest in the Sherry-Freitas Company, a large concern that sold dairy products in San Francisco under the trade name of
"Sherreitas Butter." He sat on the board of directors of the Bank of Italy
(now the Bank of American National Trust and Savings Association, the big-
gest bank in the United States), having been chosen by A.P. Giannini, the
Itlaian immigrant founder, as one of the original fifteen directors.

In 1923 the "dairying magnate" of San Rafael owned six dairy ranches.
He had become a land baron. The Freitas home place, the old Lucas Ranch,
which he bought in 1898 for $80,000 was 1,200 acres. He also owned the

1,116-acre Upper Ranch in Lucas valley, the 325-acre Butcher Ranch, the
Black Point Ranch on Atherton Road, and a ranch in Cordelia, Solano county.
His C Ranch at Novato covered 2,000 acres. The ranch house was a twenty-
six room Victorian mansion, and here the family spent a part of every year.
There was another house, in San Rafael, which the family occupied during
the months when the children attended the local Catholic schools.

On 900 acres of the Freitas home place, the town of Terra Linda was
built for 15,000 people, as were the Northgate Shopping Center and the Northgate Industrial Park. When the developers were looking for a name for their
subdivision, the Freitas daughter, Rose (Mrs. Rose F. Rose), suggested
the Portuguese words for Lovely Land. That is how Terra Linda was baptized. The Manuel T. Freitas Parkway, the main avenue of Terra Linda,
would strike anybody familiar with the saga of the dynamic man from the
Azores as aptly named, too.

Maria Bettencourt Freitas preceded her famous husband in death. This
quiet, unassuming woman, who taught her husband how to read and write,
died from cancer in 1919, at the age of forty. Manuel T. Freitas followed
her to the grave on September 12, 1923. The penniless immigrant from
São Jorge left an estate valued at one million, pre-inflationary dollars.

The couple had eight children. Edward died young. A daughter, Mrs.
Marie Freitas Crane, died in 1956. The survivors in 1974 were Manuel T.
Freitas, Jr., former Marin County Superior Court Judge Carlos R. Freitas,
Attorney Walter F. Freitas, Mrs. Rose F. Rose, Mrs. Helen F. Tichenor,
and Louis C. Freitas, the latter an ex-newspaperman and a retired school
teacher. The Freitas progeny did not sully the father's image. One of the
sons, Carlos R. Freitas, added particular lustre to it.

Judge Freitas was born in Marin county on February 7, 1904. After
graduating from St. Mary's College of California, he studied law at The
Catholic University of America, Washington, D.C., and later at Lincoln University, San Francisco. He was admitted to the state bar on August 19, 1925,
and in time to the bar of the United States Supreme Court.

He is the senior partner of the law firm of Freitas, Allen, McCarthy,
Bettini, and MacMahon of San Rafael. Formerly a judge of the Superior Court
of California for the county of Marin, he has been vice president of the State
Bar of California (1964-1965) and served it in other capacities. He is a past
president of the Marin County Bar Association.

From 1968-1970, he was president of the board of regents, St. Mary's
College, Moraga. He has served on the boards of directors or of trustees
of the Marin County Savings and Loan Association and the Marin County Financial Corporation. He is a member of the Commonwealth Club of San Francisco and of the Irmandade do Divino Espírito Santo (I.D.E.S.). He was Supreme President of the I.D.E.S. in 1928-1929. In 1942-1944, he saw service with the Office of Strategic Services in Moçambique, Portuguese East
Africa. Finally, the Portuguese government bestowed upon him, as a public
tribute for a distinguished career, the rank of commander in the Order of
Prince Henry the Navigator.

The achievements of Manuel Teixeira Freitas and of his issue point up the absurdity of classifying immigrants without formal education, or with little formal education, as "unskilled." What was once considered important was to grow up in a good society, as the ancients used to say, but the Immigration Service has obviously never paid any attention to the simple tenets of Greek wisdom.

THE BORBA FAMILY

Source: Unpublished text by Mary Borba Parente,
Ontario, California, December 10, 1974, edited by
Manoel da Silveira Cardozo.

Pete António Borba, the youngest of six children, was born on June 29,
1895, in São Tomé, Topo, São Jorge, Azores. This well-known rancher who
made his fortune in the Chino valley of Southern California was an independent and aggressive boy of sixteen when he first set foot on the soil of California. This was in 1911. He had a relative in San Luis Obispo who found
him work on a ranch where he milked cows. Having less than a year of
schooling and arriving in America with only four patacas in his pocket (besides still owing his fare) was no detriment to the pursuit of his goals in
life: success and happiness. In 1912 his restlessness took him to Imperial
valley where he worked on the railroad by day and milked cows early morning and late at night.

In 1915 he moved to Lemoore, and by the time he was nineteen he
had already acquired his first dairy. It was here that he had the good fortune of meeting his wife, Maria Ávila, born March 19, 1899, in Silveira,
Pico, Azores. She was nineteen, beautiful, and the epitome of the "strong
woman" mentioned in the Bible. They were married in 1918 and she gave
birth to their first two sons, Pete (1919) and Joseph (1920). She and their
children were the greatest assets that Pete acquired during his lifetime.
In the first year of marriage she made $500 by raising turkeys besides
working alongside her husband milking cows and in the fields.

The cold climate of the San Joaquim valley was not very agreeable
to Mr. Borba so that when he heard that people in the south were making
more money he decided that he and his family, after a new sojourn in the
scalding Imperial valley, would finally settle in milder Southern California.
It was 1924 and life was a great challenge. Here their third child, John,
was born (1927). On the day that she gave birth to her third son this formi-
dable woman milked twenty-four cows by hand.

News of a fatally ill mother caused them to return to the Azores.
During this period Mr. Borba became seriously ill and his life was barely
spared. After his recovery they returned to Chino where life began anew.
Two more children, George (1932) and Mary (1935), were born. It was
during the time of the depression but parents and children worked to accumu-
late the wealth that these two peasants had always dreamed of leaving their
children. In 1938, Mr. Borba purchased his first ranch, of 120 acres. It
was the first step to his great purchases of real estate. A neighbor recalls
that this was a sandy dune-like piece of virgin soil. Mr. Borba, using the
experience in farming that he had brought from São Jorge, covered the land
with a thick layer of manure, worked it to the best of his knowledge, and
planted potatoes that yielded a crop never before seen in the fertile Chino

valley. This crop and an easement to the Edison Company paid for the ranch in one year.

Mr. Borba proceeded with his wife and small sons to purchase and work acre after acre. Pete and Joe used to milk cows and do chores before going to school in the morning, as did John and George as they grew old enough to help. Each time that Mr. Borba bought a new piece of property his farmer peers felt that he would never make it. Once, when his banker refused to loan Pete money to purchase a 400-acre ranch, he stomped out telling the man, "You know as much about my business as I know about yours." He went to his friend, Adolph Weinberg, who helped him procure the loan, and changed banks. In retrospect, he always said that he had been a fortunate man. By 1945 the family had amassed well over 1,300 acres of land, parcels of great value on the present market.

In 1963 the family decided to divide a good portion of the land into equal shares so that each child could develop his own business. Pete, Jr., who had invested family money in the Ontario Savings and Loan Association and was on its board of directors, died unfortunately in 1965. This was the most tragic incident in the life of this family. All who knew him recognized that he was the personification of kindness, loyalty, and success rendered through hard work.

The other children of this family continue on the road to success. Joseph is part-owner of the Chino Grain and Milling Company and has expanded his dairy to over 1,200 cows, not speaking of other land investments. John and George have continued in the dairy-farming operation and are the originators of a charter issued to the Chino Valley Bank in August, 1974. George is the president of the board. Mary, the only girl in the family, married Luís Parente, a Portuguese naval officer, who has also become a dairy farmer and operates a large dairy in the same area.

Mr. Borba's optimism and intuition were staggering, and his generous spirit was admired by many. This last trait led him to give welfare to anyone who sought his help. In recognition of his good works, the Portuguese government, in 1953, bestowed upon him a medal of honor, Medalha de Benemerência.

Maria Borba worked and enjoyed working until the last days of her life. She died at the City of Hope of leukemia on August 30, 1970. Pete died suddenly on September 7, 1973. The memories of these great people serve as an example to all Portuguese immigrants who have come to seek a new life in America.

WILLIAM L. PEREIRA

Source: This text is based on the following:
Who's Who in America (1972-1973); curricu-
lum vitae supplied by Kay Wornell, Executive
Assistant to the Chairman of the Board, William
L. Pereira Associates, Los Angeles.

William L. Pereira is internationally known and respected as an architect and city planner, a giant in his field, but not many people realize, in this
nation of immigrants, that he is of Portuguese descent. It would not be difficult to guess it from his surname, if our antennas were disposed to receive
signals in Portuguese.

Born in Chicago on April 25, 1909, he graduated from the University of
Illinois in 1930 and immediately began his extraordinary career. He was a
partner in Pereira and Luckman, an architectural and engineering firm,
1950-1958. Since 1958 he has had his own firm, William L. Pereira Associates, with offices in several cities but with headquarters in Los Angeles.

Among the significant complexes that he has designed or planned have
been Cape Canaveral, CBS Television City, Union Oil Center, Los Angeles
Museum of Art, the thirty-three block Houston Center, African Riviera (Ivory
Coast), New England Center for Continuing Education, Central Library of
the University of California at San Diego, Occidental Center, the Crocker
Citizens National Bank Building in Los Angeles, and an urban center in Tai-
pei, Taiwan. He was the master planner for the Los Angeles International
Airport, Irvine Ranch, Mountain Park, University of California campus at
Irvine, University of Southern California, Catalina Island, and Abidjan, Ivory
Coast. He prepared a comprehensive development plan for the Burlington
Northern Railroad holdings in the United States and Canada.

He is a member of the advisory committee of the board of directors,
Crocker Citizens National Bank. He was on the President's National Council on the Arts, 1965-1968. In 1967-1968, he served as chairman of the California Governor's Transporation Task Force. In 1969 he was an adviser to
the Aerospace and Space Engineering Board.

He has received over twenty-four honor and merit awards from the
American Institute of Architects, the rank of commander in the Order of the
Ivory Coast for his work in developing the master plan for Abidjan. In 1940
he received the Scarab Medal, in 1942 an Oscar from the Academy of Motion
Picture Arts and Sciences (of which he is a fellow). The Humanitarian Medal
came in 1942 too, the citation from the Museum of Modern Art in 1944, the
Philadelphia Art Alliance award in 1948, and the Man of the Year award of
the Los Angeles Chamber of Commerce in 1967. In 1971, a distinction that
may have pleased him most, he was the architect in residence at the American Academy, Rome. In 1973, he was honored by the University of Illinois
School of Architecture as one of the outstanding alumni of the year. He is

a fellow of the Gargoyle Society. He has honorary doctorates from the Otis Art Institute of Los Angeles, the Art Center College of Design of Los Angeles, and Pepperdine University of Malibu.

This record of achievement, related here in its barest outline, is certainly enough to make us share the opinion held by many notable Californians, that Mr. Pereira is one of the outstanding living Americans of Portuguese ancestry.

AMARAL CIRCLE

Source: Feature story by Kitty Archibald,
Tri-Valley Herald (Livermore, California),
November 9, 1974.

John James Amaral, whose parents migrated to the United States from
the Azores to find a better life, was born and raised in New England. [Rhode
Island] He was a farm boy during his early years, and he helped with the
family's dairy before he got in his 1924 Hudson Brougham, and started across
the country to visit relatives in the Amador-Livermore Valley.

That was over fifty years ago, and Amaral is still here. He has spent
a half a century working for and with his community, but it is the fact he
has two streets named after him that leads to his being nationally recognized. . . .

It only took one telephone call to discover Amaral Circle [in Pleasanton]
was named after John J. Amaral back in 1951 when he completed development of a small tract of houses just off Kottinger Drive. It also turned out
the reigning brass of the Army's old Camp Parks had named the main street
in that military installation Amaral Avenue because of an appreciation for
the man and his devotion to his work.

Along with a thriving real estate business, Amaral not only belonged to
nearly every civic, social or fraternal organization in town, he also served
as the city's fire chief, served on a war-time deferrment board, and headed
up the county's Farm Labor Office, producing food and fiber for the war effort during the early 1940s. He was also on the Selective Service Board and
formed the local U.S.A. . . .

He went into the real estate business in 1936, the last year of his four
year term on the city council. Amaral was a member of the Pleasanton
Volunteer Fire Department from 1925 to 1960, and served in the capacity
of Fire Chief from 1940 until 1960, when he gave it all up because he had
moved outside the city limits to a new home in Castlewood Country Club.

During his thirty-five years with the fire department he belonged to
the National, California, and Intermountain Fire Chiefs Associations, started
the Pleasanton Junior Chamber of Commerce and went on to the Chamber
of Commerce where he has served as secretary for nearly thirty years and
holds a Life Membership, joined and served in various positions with the
Lions Club, also a Life Member, and the Elks Club.

Since 1928 Amaral has been secretary to the Portuguese organization
IDES -- translated means the Holy Ghost Brotherhood of California: he has
served on the Republican Assembly District 13, and on the Republican State
Central Committee with Earl Warren, former governor and Supreme Court
Justice who died last year.

The Amarals have two sons. Lee, an attorney who chose to stay in the
valley and pursue his career, and Jim, an artist, makes his home in Colom-

bia, South America, but is currently spending a year in Paris, working and studying.

If it sounds like John James Amaral has spent a lifetime working, he has, but nearly everything he has done has been for the betterment of the people, the organizations, and the community he lives in.

DR. CARLOS FERNANDES

Source: This text is based on the following: A
Colónia Portuguesa (Oakland), I, No. 81 (December 23, 1924); Portugal na Califórnia (n.p.), Special Edition (September, 1935); José Maria Ferreira de Castro, A volta ao mundo (Lisbon, 1942),
pp. 610-611.

Dr. Carlos Fernandes, born eighty-one years ago on the island of Madeira, is a graduate of the School of Medicine of the University of Lisbon.
He studied law even as he was pursuing his medical training. After graduation, he went into banking and set up a wine-exporting business that col-
lapsed when France imposed tariff restrictions on Portuguese wines. He
visited Angola in connection with his business ventures.

There was a steady stream of immigration from his island to the United
States, and the success stories of Madeirans in their new homeland inevitably
aroused his interest. Before settling in California, he visited America on
four occasions. The first visit was in 1918.

Following his business reverses, he was named consul of Portugal in
Oakland, California. He opened the first consulate on Foothill Boulevard,
whose name, as a courtesy to his office, was changed to Lisbon Avenue.

When he decided to make his home permanently in California, he began
the practice of medicine. His first offices were in the old Morton Hospital,
at 1055 Pine Street, San Francisco, maintained as a private hospital by a
corporation whose president Dr. Fernandes later became. In time the hospital's name was changed to St. John's, and under this name it became especially well-known among the Portuguese people of California.

Dr. Fernandes left the consular service of his country to devote himself to his medical and other interests. He acquired landed property in San
Francisco, Oakland, and north of the bay area. He also served for a number
of years as honorary consul of Brazil.

He played an active role, before his retirement, in Portuguese civic affairs in California, and was in great demand as a public speaker. His hospi-
tality was proverbial, and he became the unofficial ambassador of Portugal
in San Francisco. He was likewise a successful practitioner of the medical
and surgical arts.

His daughter is married to Dr. Francisco M. Soares Silva, of San Rafael, the author of a doctoral dissertation on the Azorean poet Antero de
Quental (1842-1891).

PORTUGUESE IMMIGRATION TO THE UNITED STATES
1820-1972

Source: U.S. Immigration and Naturalization Service, Annual Report, 1965, p. 48; U.S. Bureau of the Census, Statistical abstract of the United States, 1973, 94th ed., p. 95.

Grand total: 379,130

1821 - 1830	145
1831 - 1840	829
1841 - 1850	550
1851 - 1860	1,055
1861 - 1870	2,658
1871 - 1880	14,082
1881 - 1890	16,089
1891 - 1900	27,508
1901 - 1910	69,149
1911 - 1920	89,732
1921 - 1930	29,994
1931 - 1940	3,329
1941 - 1950	7,423
1951 - 1960	19,588
1961 - 1970	76,065
1971 - 1972	20,010

MISCELLANEOUS STATISTICS

Source: U.S. Bureau of the Census, Statistical abstract of the United States, 1973, 94th ed., pp. 98; 100; Instituto Nacional de Estatistica (Portugal), Anuario estatistico, 1972, pp. 23-24.

1954-1972   Portuguese refugees admitted to the United States, 5,001

1960   Portuguese aliens under Alien Address Program, 32,000

1970   Portuguese aliens under Alien Address Program, 81,000

1972   Portuguese aliens under Alien Address Program, 102,000

1970   Total emigration from the Azores, 4,319

                    to Canada, 2,225
                    to America, 1,961

1970   Emigration from Portugal to Canada, 1,136

1970   Emigration from Portugal to the United States, 1,906

BIBLIOGRAPHY

Adams, Romanzo. The Peoples of Hawaii. Honolulu: American Council,
Institute of Pacific Relations, 1933.

Agostinho, José. "Um emigrante açoriano José Gonçalves Correia, " Boletim
do Instituto Histórico da Ilha Terceira (Angra do Heroísmo, Terceira,
Azores), X, 1-35.

Aguiar, Armando de. O mundo que os portugueses criaram. Lisboa, 1954.

Alcoforado, Francisco. An Historical Account of the Discovery of the Island
of Madeira, Abridged from the Portuguese Original, To Which Is Added,
An Account of the Present State of the Island, in a Letter to a Friend.
London, 1950.

Alden, Dauril. "Yankee Sperm Whalers in Brazilian Waters, and the Decline
of the Portuguese Whale Fishery (1773-1801), " The Americas (Washington, D. C.), XX, no. 3 (January, 1964), 267-288.

Almeida, Carlos. "António Fonte pai ou padrinho?!..., " U.P.E.C. Life
(San Leandro, California), LXIX, no. 3 (July, 1970), 3, 5-6, 8, 14.

_____. "Men in Our Country, " U.P.E.C. Life (San Leandro, Califor-
nia), LXX, no. 2 (April, 1971), 4.

Andrade, Laurinda C. The Open Door. New Bedford, Massachusetts: Privately printed, 1968.

Andrade, Margarette de. Brazilian Cookery Traditional and Modern (Rut-
land, Vermont: Charles E. Tuttle Co., 1965).

Baron, Salo Wittmayer. A Social and Religious History of the Jews. Second
edition, revised and enlarged. Vol. XV. New York and Philadelphia, 1973.

Barrow, John. A Chronological History of Voyages into the Arctic Regions;
Undertaken Chiefly for the Purpose of Discovering a North-east, Northwest, or Polar Passage Between the Atlantic and Pacific: From the Earliest Periods of Scandinavian Navigation, to the Departure of the Recent
Expeditions, under the Orders of Captains Ross and Buchan. London,
1818. (Reprinted by Barnes & Noble, Inc., New York, 1971, with an introduction by Christopher Lloyd.)

Beazley, Charles Raymond. John and Sebastian Cabot the Discovery of North
America. New York 1967? (First published, London, 1898.)

Benavides, Afonso de. Benavides' Memorial of 1630. Translated by Peter P. Forrestal. With an historical introduction and notes by Cyprian J. Lynch. Publications of the Academy of American Franciscan History Documentary Series, 2. Washington, D. C.: Academy of American Franciscan History, 1954.

Biddle, Anthony Joseph Drexel. The Land of the Wine Being An Account of the Madeira Islands at the Beginning of the Twentieth Century, and from a New Point of View. 2 vols. Philadelphia: Drexel Biddle, 1901.

—————. The Madeira Islands. Vol. I. Philadelphia, 1900.

Bohme, Frederick G. "The Portuguese in California," California Historical Quarterly, September, 1956.

Boxer, Charles Ralph. "Portuguese and Spanish Rivalry in the Far East During the Seventeenth Century," Journal of the Royal Asiatic Society, December, 1946, and April, 1947, pp. 150-164, 91-105, respectively.

Brazilian American Cultural Institute. A Survey of the Portuguese Language, Luso Brazilian and Latin American Area Studies in Institutions of Higher Learning in the United States. Washington, D. C., 1974.

Cabeza de Vaca, Alvar Núñex. Naufragios y comentarios con dos cartas. Second edition. Colección Austral, 304. Buenos Aires: Espasa-Calpe Argentina, S.A., 1946.

Cardozo, Manoel da Silveira, ed. Catalog of the Oliveira Lima Library The Catholic University of America Washington, D.C. 2 vols. Boston: G. K. Hall & Co., 1970.

—————. "A Presença de Portugal nos Estados Unidos," Boletim do Instituto Histórico da Ilha Terceira (Angra do Heroísmo, Terceira, Azores), XVI, 9-19.

Carlos, José. Padres da ilha do Pico alunos no Seminário Episcopal de Angra subsídios biográficos. Vol. I. Turlock, California: Privately printed , 1970.

Castro, A.D. "The Portuguese in Hawaii," The Mid-Pacific Magazine, VIII, no. 1. (July, 1914), 53-57.

Castro, José Maria Ferreira de. A volta ao mundo. Lisboa, 1942.

Cavaco, Gilbert R. Luso-Brazilian Studies Survey the Teaching of Portuguese in the United States Academic Year 1969-1970. Fall River, Massachusetts: Luso-Brazilian Studies Survey, 1974. 2 vols.

Cavazos Garza, Israel. Cedulario Autobiográfico de Pobladores y Conquis-
tadores de Nuevo León. Biblioteca de Nuevo León, 2. Monterrey, México, 1964.

Chapman, Charles Edward. A History of California: The Spanish Period.
New York, 1921.

Columbus, Christopher. Los cuatro viajes del almirante y su testamento.
Edited by Ignacio B. Anzoátegui. Colección Austral, 633. Buenos Aires:
Espasa-Calpe Argentina, S.A., 1946.

Corrêa, Alberto. "Ensaios sobre a história da imprensa portuguesa" and
"Jornais portugeses publicados na California, " Jornal Português (Oakland,
California), October 3, 1958.

Cortesão, Jaime. Os portugueses no descobrimento dos Estados Unidos.
Lisboa, 1949.

Costa, Euclides Goulart da. Portugal descobridor apontamentos respeitantes
à descoberta da Califórnia. Lixboa, 1928.

Coutinho, Helen. Pleasant Recollections of Dr. Joaquim de Siqueira Coutinho.
New York: Saint Anthony Press, 1969.

Cross, Ira B. Financing an Empire History of Banking in California. Chicago, San Francisco, Los Angeles: The S.J. Clarke Publishing Co., 1927.

Davis, Richard Beale. "The Abbé Correa in America, 1812-1820 - the Contributions of the Diplomat and Natural Philosopher to the Foundations of
Our National Life. Correspondence with Jefferson and Other Members
of the American Philosophical Society and with Other Prominent Americans, " Transactions of the American Philosophical Society (Philadelphia),
new series, XLV, part 2 (May, 1955), 87-197.

Dawson, Samuel Edward. "The Voyages of the Cabots Latest Phases of the
Controversy, " Royal Society of Canada, III (1897), section II, 139 et seq.

Day, A. Grove. Coronado's Quest The Discovery of the Southeastern States.
Berkeley and Los Angeles: University of California Press, 1940.

Denny, J.O. Financial California: An Historical Review of the Beginnings
and Progress of Banking in the State. (San Francisco: The Coast Banker
Publishing Co., 1916.)

deShara, Walter. "Group from Madeira Islands Settled in Jacksonville, Illinois, 102 Years Ago, " Standard-Times (New Bedford, Massachusetts),
May 20, 1951.

Dias, Eduardo Mayone. "A imigração portuguesa na Califórnia," Seara Nova no. 1515 (January, 1972), 11-15.

_____. "A Presença Portuguesa na Califórnia," Jornal Português (Oakland, California), August 23-October 18, 1973.

Dos Passos, John, The Portugal Story: Three Centuries of Exploration and Discovery. Garden City, New York: Doubleday & Co., Inc., 1969.

Duncan, T. Bentley. Atlantic Islands Madeira, the Azores and the Cape Verdes in the Seventeenth-Century Commerce and Navigation. Chicago: The University of Chicago Press, 1972.

Elbert, Samuel H., and Edgar C. Knowlton, Jr., "Ukulele," American Speech, XXXII, no. 4 (December, 1957), 307-310.

Estep, George A. "Portuguese Assimilation in Hawaii and California," Sociology and Social Research, XXVI, no. 1 (September-October, 1941), 61-69.

Florentino, Nicolau, pseudonym for António Maria de Freitas, and Regina Maney. The Wife of Columbus, with Genealogical Tree of the Perestrello and Moniz Families. New York, 1893.

Fowler, John. Journal of a Tour in the State of New York, in the Year 1840; with Remarks on Agriculture; and Return to England by the Western Islands, in Consequence of Shipwreck in the Robert Fulton. London, 1831.

Frankfurter, Felix. "Benjamin Nathan Cardozo," Dictionary of American Biography, XXII, supplement 2. New York, 1958. pp. 93-96.

Freitas, Joaquim Francisco. Portuguese-American Memories. Hawaii, 1930.

Gracia, Frances Sylvia. Early Portuguese Settlers in Little Compton, Rhode Island. Little Compton, Rhode Island: Privately printed, 1974.

Graves, Alvin R. "The Portuguese in California, 1850-1880: A Geographical Analysis of Early Settlement Phenomena," U.P.E.C. Life (San Leandro, California), LXXIII, no. 3 (July, 1974), 4-7.

Guill, James H. A History of the Azores. Atherton, California: Privately printed, 1974.

Gutstein, Morris Aaron. Aaron Lopez and Judah Touro A Refugee and a Son of a Refugee. New York: Behrman's Jewish Book House, 1939.

_____. The Story of the Jews of Newport Two and a Half Centuries of Judaism 1658-1908. New York: Bloch Publishing Co., 1938.

H. D. Ensayo de Historia Patria Obra adaptada a los Programas vigentes de Bachillerato y de Estudios Magisteriales. Vol. I, ninth edition. Montevideo, 1950.

Hakluyt, Richard. The Principal Navigations Voyages Traffiques & Discoveries of the English Nation Made by Sea or Overland to the Remote and Farthest Distant Quarters of the Earth at Any Time Within the Compass of These 1600 Years. 8 vols. New York: E.P. Dutton & Co., 1927.

_____. The Voyages Traffiques and Discoveries of Foreign Voyages with Other Matters Relating Thereto Contained in the "Navigations." 2 vols. New York: E.P. Dutton & Co., 1928.

Halliwell, Leslie. The Filmgoer's Companion. New York, 1966.

Hanke, Lewis. The Portuguese in Spanish America, with Special Reference to the Villa Imperial de Potosi. N.p., n.d.

Harrisse, Henry. John Cabot the Discoverer of North America and Sebastian His Son: A Chapter of the Maritime History of England Under the Tudors 1496-1557. New York: Argosy-Antiquarian, Ltd., 1968. (First printed in 1896.)

Hoffman, Frederic L. "The Portuguese Population in the United States," Quarterly Publications of the American Statistical Association, new series, no. 47, vol. VI (September, 1899), 327-336.

Holmes, Jr., Urban Tigner. "Portuguese Americans," in Francis J. Brown and Joseph Slabey Roucek, eds., Our Racial and National Minorities Their History, Contributions, and Present Problems. New York: Prentice-Hall, Inc., 1937. Pp. 394-405.

Hughes, T. M. The Ocean Flower; a Poem. Preceded by An Historical and Descriptive Account of the Island of Madeira, a Summary of the Discoveries and Chivalrous History of Portugal and an Essay on Portuguese Literature. London, 1845.

Instituto Nacional de Estatistica. Anuário demográfico 1966. Lisboa, n.d.

_____. Anuário estatístico 1972. Lisboa, n.d.

Jensen, John B. "The Portuguese Immigrant Community of New England: A Current Look," Stvdia (Lisboa), no. 34 (June, 1972), 109-151.

Journal of the House of Representatives of the Twentieth Legislature of the Territory of Hawaii Regular Session, 1939. Honolulu, 1939.

Keith, Henry H. "New World Interlopers: The Portuguese in the Spanish West Indies, From the Discovery to 1640, " The Americas (Washington, D.C.), XXX 91969), 360-371.

Knowlton, Edgar C., Jr. "Portuguese in Hawaii, " Kentucky Foreign Language Quarterly (Lexington, Kentucky), VII, 212-218.

_____. "The Portuguese Language Press of Hawaii, " Social Process in Hawaii, XXVI (1960), 89-99.

. "Portuguese Language Resources for Hawaiian History, " Hawaiian Historical Society Seventieth Annual Report for the Year 1961. Honolulu, 1962. pp. 24-37.

Lagoa, Visconde de. João Rodrigues Cabrilho. Lisboa, 1958.

Lai, Kum Pui. "Hawaiian Minority Groups, " in Francis J. Brown and Joseph Slabey Roucek, eds., Our Racial and National Minorities Their History, Contributions, and Present Problems. New York: Prentice-Hall, Inc., 1937. pp. 525-534.

Lang, Henry R. "The Portuguese Element in New England, " The Journal of American Folk-Lore, V (1892), 9-18.

Lewis, Alfred. Home Is an Island. New York: Random House, 1951.

Lima, Gervásio. Frei Gonçalo Velho o descobridor dos Açores, seu retrato e de sua casa e Igreja em Santa Maria. Angra do Heroísmo, Terceira, Azores (1926).

Lind, Andrew William. Hawaii's People. Third edition. Honolulu: University of Hawaii Press, 1967.

Lingg, Ann M. John Philip Sousa. New York, 1954.

Lopes, Francisco Fernandes. Os irmãos Corte-Real. Centro de Estudos Históricos Ultramarinos, Lisboa: Agência Geral do Ultramar, 1937.

Maltzberger, Elma. The Story of Colton, California. Colton, California, 1974.

Marques, A.J. "The Portuguese in Hawaii, " Thrum's Hawaiian Annual (Honolulu, 1911).

BIBLIOGRAPHY

Mazzatenta, O. Louis. "New England's 'Little Portugal,'" National Geographic (Washington, D.C.), vo. 147, no. 1 (January, 1975), 90-109.

Morison, Samuel Eliot. Admiral of the Ocean Sea A Life of Christopher Columbus. Vol. I. New York: Time, Inc., 1962.

_____. The European Discovery of America: The Northern Voyages A.D. 500-1600. New York: Oxford University Press, 1971.

Neistein, José, and Manoel Cardozo. Poesia brasileira moderna: A Bilingual Anthology. Washington, D.C.: Brazilian-American Cultural Institute, 1972.

Oliver, Lawrence. Never Backward: The Autobiography of Lawrence Oliver a Portuguese-American. Edited by Rita Larkin Wolin. San Diego: Privately printed, 1972.

Pap, Leo. Portuguese-American Speech: An Outline of Speech Conditions Among Portuguese Immigrants in New England and Elsewhere in the United States. New York, 1949.

_____. "Portuguese Pioneers and Early Immigrants in North America," in Actas, V Coloquio Internacional de Estudos Luso-Brasileiros. Vol. I. Coimbra, 1965. pp. 5-15.

Pease, Zephaniah W. History of New Bedford. 3 vols. New York, 1918.

Pérez Maldonado, Carlos. La Civdad Metropolitana de Nvestra Señora de Monterrey. Monterrey, México, 1946.

Portugal na Califórnia (Oakland, California). Special edition, September, 1935. Under the editorial direction of Jordão Marques Jardim.

"Portuguese in America," The Literary Digest, vol. 63, November 22, 1919, 40.

Reis, Manuel, and Jack Costa. 100 Luso-American Fraternal Federation - United National Life Insurance Society. San Francisco: Luso-American Fraternal Federation [1968].

Representative Men and Old Families of Southeastern Massachusetts. Vol. III. Chicago, 1912.

Ribes Tovar, Federico. A Chronological History of Puerto Rico. New York, 1971.

Santos, M.G. Almanach Portuguez de Hawaii para 1911; um Livro de re-
    ferencia e informação Geral Relativo ao Territorio de Hawaii, Portugal,
    Madeira, e Açores. Honolulu: Companhia Editora do Pacifico, 1911.

Sanz, Carlos. Australia su descobrimiento y denominación con la reproduc-
    cion facsímil del memorial de Quirós y otras rarísimas ilustraciones.
    Madrid, 1963.

Sawyer, Eugene T. History of Santa Clara County California with Biographi-
    cal Sketches of the Leading Men and Women of the County Who Have Been
    Identified With Its Growth and Development From the Early Days to the
    Present. Los Angeles: Historic Record Company, 1922.

Schneiderman, Harry. "Jewish American," in Francis J. Brown and Joseph
    Slabey Roucek, eds., Our Racial and National Minorities Their History
    Contributions, and Present Problems. New York: Prentice-Hall, 1937.
    pp. 406-425.

Sherburne, John Henry. Life and Character of the Chevalier John Paul Jones,
    a Captain in the Navy of the United States, During Their Revolutionary
    War. Washington, D.C., 1825.

Smith, Adam. An Inquiry into the Nature and Causes of the Wealth of Na-
    tions. With an introduction by Max Lerner. New York: The Modern Li-
    brary, 1937. (First printed in 1776.)

Smith, Robert C. "A pioneer teacher: Father Peter Babad and his Portu-
    guese Grammar," Hispania (August, 1945), 330-363.

_____. "A Portuguese Naturalist in Philadelpħia, 1799," The Penn-
    sylvania Magazine of History and Biography, LXXVIII, no. 1 (January,
    1954), 71-106.

Soares, Celestino. California and the Portuguese How the Portuguese Helped
    to Build Up California: A Monograph Written for the Golden Gate Inter-
    national Exposition on San Francisco Bay 1939. Lisbon, 1939.

Sousa, John Philip. Marching Along. New York, 1925.

S.P.R.S.I. Diamond Jubilee 1898-1973 Cook Book. Oakland, California,
    1973.

Stern, Malcolm H. Americans of Jewish Descent: A Compendium of Gen-
    ealogy. Publications of the American Jewish Archives, 5. Cincinnati:
    Hebrew Union College Press, 1960.

BIBLIOGRAPHY   149

Taft, Donald R. Two Portuguese Communities in New England. New York, 1923.

Tavares, Belmira E. Portuguese Pioneers in the United States. Fall River, Massachusetts; Privately printed, 1973.

Taylor, William. California Life Illustration. New York, 1859.

Toussaint, Manuel. Colonial Art in Mexico. Translated and edited by Elizabeth Wilder Weismann. Austin: Univerzity of Texas Press. 1967.

U.S. Census. 8th Census, 1860. Population of the United States in 1860; Compiled from the Original Returns of the Eighth Census Under the Direction of the Secretary of the Interior, by Joseph C. G. Kennedy, Superintendent of Census. Washington, D.C.: Government Printing Office, 1864.

_____. 9th Census, 1870. A Compendium of the Ninth Census (June 1, 1870) Compiled Pursuant to a Concurrent Resolution of Congress and under the Direction of the Secretary of the Interior by Francis A. Walker, Superintendent of Census. Washington, D.C.: Government Printing Office, 1872.

_____. Statistical Abstract of the United States, 1973. 94th edition.

U.S. Immigration and Naturalization Service. Annual Report, 1965.

Vancouver, George. A Voyage of Discovery to the North Pacific Ocean, and Round the World: In Which the Coast of North-west America Has Been Carefully Examined and Accurately Surveyed Undertaken by His Majesty's Command. Principally with a View to Ascertain the Existence of any Navigable Communication Between the North Pacific and North Atlantic Oceans; and Performed in the Years 1790, 1791, 1792, 1793, 1794, and 1795, in the Discovery Sloop of War, and Armed Tender Chatham. New edition with corrections. Vol. V. London, 1801.

Vaz, August Mark. The Portuguese in California. Oakland, California: I.D.E.S. Supreme Council, 1965.

Wagner, Henry R. Spanish Voyages to the Northwest Coast of America in the Sixteenth Century. San Francisco, 1929.

Washington, Joseph R. Jr. Black Sects and Cults. New York, 1972.

Weinstock, Herbert. "John Philip Sousa," The Encyclopedia Americana (1970), XXV, 284-285.

Young, Nancy F., ed. The Portuguese in Hawaii a Resource Guide. Ethnic

150 THE PORTUGUESE IN AMERICA

Research and Resource Center Publication, 11. Honolulu: Hawaii Foundation for History and the Humanities, 1973.

NEWSPAPERS

Catholic Voice (Oakland, California), December 16, 1974

Colónia Portuguesa (Oakland, California), I, no. 81 (December 23, 1924).

Diário de Notícias (New Bedford, Massachusetts), 1919-1973.

Evening Outlook (Santa Monica, California), January 30, 1947.

Evening Star (Washington, D. C.), October 7, 1970.

Hayward Journal (Hayward, California), June 27, 1916.

Independent-Journal (San Rafael, California), May 25, 1974.

Jornal Português (Oakland, California), 1888-.

Luso Americano (Newark, New Jersey), 1928-.

New York Times (New York, New York), August 6, 9, 13, 14 and September 24, 1955; January 13, 1960.

Oakland Tribune (Oakland, California), January 21, 1974.

Portuguese Times (New Bedford, Massachusetts), 1972-.

Terra Linda News (Marin County, California), May 15, 1974.

Tri-Valley Herald (Livermore, California), November 9, 1974.

Voz de Portugal (Hayward, California), 1960-.

Washington Post (Washington, D. C.), January 13, 1960.